Adopted,
Transformed,
Set Free

Sabrina Martinelli

Adopted, Transformed, Set Free

Unless stated otherwise, all scripture references come from the amplified translation of the Bible, copyright 2015, The Lockman Foundation, La Habra, CA 90631.

Details in some anecdotes and stories have been changed to protect the identities of the persons involved

ISBN: 9798668965380
Imprint: Independently published

FIRST EDITION

www.fb.me/AdoptedTransformedSetFree.com

This book is dedicated to all who want to be set free.
We are not identified by who we have been with or what others have done to us.
We can be transformed. We can be set free.

CONTENTS

Character Representation

Mom & Dad - (biological parents)

Grandma H - (grandmother, Dad's mom)

Pa & Nannie - (grandparents, Mom's parents)

P.W. & Michal - (adoptive parents)

Nabal - (stepdad)

Bro. A & Miriam - (foster parents, Solomon & Samsons' adoptive parents)

Solomon - (biological brother)

Samson - (biological brother)

Mark - (biological brother)

Orpha - (biological sister)

Ananias - (adoptive brother)

Judas - (adoptive brother)

Abner - (adoptive brother)

Samaritan - (adoptive brother)

Marah - (adoptive sister)

Noadiah - (ex-boss)

1

Candace - (boss's daughter)

Martha - (boss's office assistant)

Deborah - (friend)

Ruth - (friend)

Mary - (friend)

CHAPTER ONE

The Harbinger

**"I will give thanks and praise to You, for I am
fearfully and wonderfully made."
Psalm 139:14**

When my mother was twenty years old, she
attended college and worked as a nurse's aide at a
rehabilitation hospital. While working, she met and
developed a relationship with a twenty-six-year-old
RN that quickly led to a pregnancy. This
unexpected surprise only intensified Mom's
morning sickness, basically forcing her to drop out
of college. When Mom told him she was pregnant,
my father told her to abort me. He even tried to take
her to the women's clinic for the procedure. God
obviously did not allow that to happen.

During her pregnancy, she discovered her baby's
daddy had gotten another woman pregnant at the
same time, who happened to be his high school
sweetheart, about nine weeks ahead of her. Along
with all the hormones that come with pregnancy,
many questions were raised between the two
women. When Mom confronted my Dad about it, he
told her the other woman's baby was not even his. I
cannot imagine what Dad thought about the choices
he had made and the consequences that were to

follow.

As I was in the middle of writing this book, I learned I have another half-sibling in Heaven due to an abortion when I was three or four years old. As I grew older and learned of all these circumstances, it instilled a goal in me to not get pregnant and drop out of university before I graduated.

An unplanned pregnancy was a surprise to my unwed parents, but it was no surprise to God. If you feel unwanted it is time to realize God created you and always had a plan for your existence or you would not be here. Your destiny was established long before you were conceived in your mother's womb. No longer must you believe the lie that you were not wanted or planned. You ARE wanted, you ARE needed, you ARE loved (all mishaps and mistakes included), you ARE God's plan.

CHAPTER TWO

Dad

"And the peace of God [that peace which reassures the heart, that peace] which transcends all understanding, [that peace which] stands guard over your hearts and your minds in Christ Jesus [is yours]."
Philippians 4:7

Dad had one older brother who lived with him and three step siblings; two were from his father's first marriage and the third one was from another relationship my grandfather was in before he married Grandma H, my grandmother. That third step sibling ended up dying from a drug overdose. Dad grew up Catholic and attended a Catholic school when he was little. I remember being in my grandparents' swimming pool even though I would have had to have been under five years old. I also remember the layout of their house, and I especially remember the closet that was behind the recliner in their living room, where they kept my toys.

Dad chose the wrong path in life that led to many negative consequences. He first tried marijuana at eleven years old when his older brother told him he had to smoke it, and after that his life became a living Hell. Smoking marijuana one time opened the door for him to try many other drugs. This led to a terrible, life-threatening addiction that no one could stop. He then grew up to be a rebellious teenager as he chose to mix drugs with alcohol. One drug led to another drug until he developed a strong addiction that caused him to become a full-blown drug addict.

Although he was wild and rebellious, he was incredibly intelligent in school. Many who get in trouble are usually smart people who have a bright future ahead of them. His rebellious mentality and destructive drug habits got him kicked out of high school and put in a juvenile detention center, but his intelligence got him into college before his high school class even graduated. In college he studied to become an RN, but that did not keep him from going to college parties where he gained access to even more drugs by going to frat parties. Even with a bright future with a nursing degree under his belt, Dad still had a major drug addiction. His destructive and detrimental addiction took him to death's door several times throughout his life. He landed a job working at a hospital but started stealing narcotics there resulting in multiple charges added to his record. One charge led to another charge before his addiction led him into a downhill spiral that resulted in a twenty-one-month prison sentence. Soon after he was released, he was arrested again and sentenced to another prison term of eight years and four months.

Even so, memories of Dad are wrapped up in my

childhood: I was Daddy's little girl. Mom froze pieces of my birthday cake for him every year when he could not be there, and when he was, we loved to watch Animal Planet together. We often reminisce on the time I was in the front seat of his car and somehow managed to drive it into a ditch. I still recall the time Dad escaped from jail and hid in Nannie and Pa's, my grandparents, attic until the police found him there. I will never forget watching as they put him in the back of the police car, nor will I forget his bright orange jumpsuit as we talked around a cafeteria table when Mom took me to see him in a prison.

Much later I was in a courtroom where another little girl was talking to her dad through a TV screen. He was wearing an orange jumpsuit, just like my own Dad's, a reminder of so many confusing memories. Trauma-related memories can come back to your mind when you least expect them. Learning to process and deal with the emotions attached to them will determine your emotional wellbeing for the rest of your life. Trauma cannot be swept under the rug because it will more than likely come back to you later. Bad episodic memories can be damaging, never underestimate the power of forgiveness and healing as it brings new life and restores all that was broken.

CHAPTER THREE

Mom

"For I know the plans and thoughts that I have for you,' says the Lord, 'plans for peace and well-being and not for disaster, to give you a future and a hope."
Jeremiah 29:11

Mom was the eldest of three, with one brother and one sister. She repeated many of the generational family patterns that caused her to fall into a lot of abuse (both verbal and physical) due to all the dysfunction. I have no recollection of going to church as a little kid with Mom, but my Grandma H told me I went to church with her many times when I was a baby. We all have a background with God, whether we know *about* Him, actually *know* Him, serve the *idea* of Him, or choose to *disregard* Him and His presence.

After I was born, Mom had my two little brothers, Solomon and Samson. I was five years old when Samson was born, I remember her bringing him home because I wanted to help take care of him. I especially wanted to help feed him, as I would watch her prepare his bottles. I became a little mom who was the bossy protective big sister to both of her little brothers.

I remember much more about Mom's parents than I do Dad's parents because I lived with Mom at their house. Nannie often sat between Solomon and me on her back-porch swing, peeling what seemed like a whole bag of Red Delicious apples, and gave us apple pieces that we ate faster than she could peel.

I remember the layout of Nannie and Pa's house. I remember helping Pa put a vacuum cleaner together in the middle of the living room floor when I was a little girl. I remember playing Crash Bandicoot with my uncle. And I remember my aunt climbing out of her bedroom window onto the roof to tan. She always used sticks of butter to enhance her tan. I used to have a habit of getting up in the middle of the night and going to the kitchen to eat sticks of butter out of the fridge. Nannie and my aunt also took care of me, especially while Mom was at work.

Mom's brother ended up going into rehab due to all the family dysfunction and personal choices. While there he became friends with a man named Nabal who would later become my stepdad. Mom eventually learned this man had a drinking problem that caused abusive behavior. He was the one who noticed all the dysfunction in her family and knew it was not a good environment for her children. It was Nabal who suggested they take Solomon, Samson, and me to Alabama to visit Michal, his newly married sister, who had four children.

From the time I was five years old until I was eleven, I either lived with Mom, Michal and P.W., or shuffled between foster homes. This meant I attended seven different schools between kindergarten until I graduated from high school. I was in more schools than foster homes.

Neither Mom nor Nabal had any stability. They had a car but did not always have a house, and if they did have a house, they did not live in it very long. Many nights, if they were not in a motel, they slept in their car, and there were times when my siblings and I slept in the car with them due to their instability.

CHAPTER FOUR

Sturdy Foundation

"So that Christ may dwell in your hearts through your faith. And may you, having been [deeply] rooted and [securely] grounded in love"
Ephesians 3:17

Stability is vital for children. Without stability children often carry the weight of their parents' responsibilities on their shoulders, some even blame themselves for their parents' inadequacies. This unfair burden is too heavy for a child to carry, as it weighs on them and causes anxiety. Fear shapes the mindset of a child, blocking them from the peace of God. Whatever is planted in a young child's mind develops roots and strongholds that, if not addressed early, are difficult to uproot when they grow into adulthood.

God entrusts parents with children to raise in His perfect love. Parents will never be perfect; as humans we are fallible. Many children grow up feeling as if no one loves them simply because no one ever emphasized the love Christ has for them. The love of a parent, boyfriend, girlfriend, friend, sibling, or spouse is not enough. This is why it is so important to teach a child about the love of Christ. God's love is infallible.

All too often, parents do not teach their children about the love of Jesus because they themselves have found a false validation in something other than Jesus Christ. True validation only comes from the pure, undefiled love of Christ.

God never intended for a child to have to play the role of the parent. Children should never have to worry about their parents' provision, but an unbalanced family structure puts too much responsibility on the child. Many children are forced to take the lead in the home because their parents never learned how to deal with their personal pain and brokenness brought on from their own childhood trauma, making it difficult to be an effective parent.

Parents cannot be good ministers of the Gospel if they do not first allow God to heal the pains of their past. It is important to learn how to deal with their trauma, so they do not parent out of the brokenness of an unhealed and unforgiving heart. We cannot pour out something that has not first been poured into us. Hurt people hurt more people, and brokenness can be detected by the fruit their character produces.

Those who have done the work to be healed can relate and minister to the broken, but only God can change them, and change does not come until we are ready to do so. Those who have not addressed the pains of the past, but claim they are whole and healed, usually end up revealing their brokenness through their insecurities. We must allow God to heal our wounds if we desire to be set free from whatever has damaged us.

Children are more likely to imitate the behavior and actions of their parents than they are to listen and obey their instructions. When they see their parents do something they are told not to do, it causes the child to question their parent's credibility. If a parent chooses to smoke, drink, sleep around, cuss, worry, or panic in a crisis, the door is opened for their child to experience the same addictions and trauma they learn from witnessing all their parents do. Why give the child a reason to call the parent a hypocrite?

Words are powerful, but our actions always speak louder than words. Taking a child to church every Sunday does not do much good if we neglect to first show them the character and image of Jesus inside of your own home. Are we perfect? No, but if we want our children to love and pursue Jesus, they need to witness your love and pursuit of Jesus with their own eyes. Why would they want to follow Jesus if their parents are following money, status, and whatever their flesh desires? Our hearts follow whatever we treasure. Too many parents depend on the church to raise their children to love Jesus when they themselves cannot turn their television off long enough for a family devotion to teach their children about the Bible.

The Word of God makes us wise, but if we neglect it, we may be tempted to fill our minds and hearts with things that contradict the wisdom and instruction of God. If your kids see you living a compromised lifestyle, why should they not follow in the same footsteps?

Just as God will judge pastors for how they shepherd their flocks, God will also judge parents for how they choose to raise their children. *"Train up a child in the way he should go [teaching him to seek God's wisdom and will for his abilities and talents], Even when he is old, he will not depart from it."* (Pro. 22:6)

It is far from wise to parent our children as Eli did in the Bible. He knew his children were rebellious but, instead of setting Biblical standards for his sons to adhere to, Eli chose to turn his head in the other direction. Parents who neglect to teach their children the wisdom of God hardly value the gifts God has already placed within their children.

Children do not come into their full potential until they develop an intimate relationship with the Holy Spirit. After Jesus resurrected from dying on the cross, the Holy Spirit was sent to guide and direct us along the path that God designed for us to walk.

CHAPTER FIVE

Medical Emergency

**"God is our refuge and strength [mighty and
impenetrable],
A very present and well-proved help in trouble."
Psalm 46:1**

My siblings and I stayed with Michal and P.W.
while Mom and Nabal went out to find the stability
they needed to provide care for us. While there,
Solomon had a major medical situation that the
hospital could not treat without the signature of one
of his biological parents. For a time, between his
prison terms, Dad came back into the picture and
gave consent for the hospital to treat Solomon for
scarlet fever. This was also the first time I met
Mark, my half-brother who is nine weeks older than
me.This medical crisis without our mom brought on
an entirely new set of problems as we were taken
into the custody of the state of Alabama. With
Michal and P.W.'s own four children (Ananias,
Judas, Abner, and Marah) and our sibling group of
four (Solomon, Samson, Orpah and myself), the
state declared there were too many children under
one roof. So, in order to keep all eight children
under one roof, their home had to legally become a
group home
    Children are rarely placed for immediate

adoption when they are put into foster care. Infants are usually the first to be placed for adoption because most foster parents desire to adopt a baby. Since many foster parents fear an older child has already experienced personal trauma, older kids are harder to place. Teenagers are the biggest challenge to find placement in the foster system. Many teens choose to rebel due to all the trauma they have experienced through losing their biological parents, forcing them to grow up in the foster care system. Most rare of all is for a foster family to take an entire sibling group of various ages at the same time, so my three siblings and I were extremely blessed to be placed together within the same family.

CHAPTER SIX

Foster Care

**"To set free those who are oppressed
(downtrodden, bruised, crushed by tragedy)."
Luke 4:18**

Sexual Abuse

When I was a little girl, P.W. exposed himself
to me. I was too young and naive at the time to
realize this is a form of sexual abuse. I still
remember the camouflage pants he wore, where it
happened, how he was sitting, and how he was
acting. It was all a very traumatic experience for
me.

It is common for many who experience any kind
of emotional, psychological, physical, or sexual
abuse to hang on to painful memories created by
such a traumatic event, whether we want to
remember or not. To properly heal from the abuse,
it is important to acknowledge the pain that the
negative experience imprinted on our brain. If not,
we push it down so far we become numb; instead of
dealing with the trauma, we have put ourselves in
an emotional prison.

If you are like me, you may think that allowing
yourself to become numb from the pain shows how

truly strong you are. This is a false and deceptive perspective that only leads to greater pain and possibly more trauma. One reason why I love Jesus is because He sets the captives free. When Jesus sets us free, we have no need to fear pain or falling back into the bondage caused by trauma. Now we are free to be who God created us to be.

Our identity is not in who we have been or what people have done to us. There is absolutely no condemnation for those who are in Christ. *"Therefore there is now no condemnation [no guilty verdict, no punishment] for those who are in Christ Jesus [who believe in Him as personal Lord and Savior]."* (Rom. 8:1)

God can set us free from trauma, but not until we understand that our identity was determined before the very foundation of the world: … *"Just as [in His love] He chose us in Christ [actually selected us for Himself as His own] before the foundation of the world, so that we would be holy [that is, consecrated, set apart for Him, purpose-driven] and blameless in His sight. In love."* (Eph. 1:4) Identity can only be found in Christ because He created us in His own image.

When P.W. exposed himself, he acted like a pervert and did not say anything to me. I suppose he was waiting to see my reaction to his disgusting sexual behavior. Although I was young, I had enough sense to run away, but I never told anyone.

P.W. had exposed himself to me even though he sat on a church pew every Sunday and occasionally played guitar while my siblings and I sang on the stage for the church congregation. Growing up,

P.W. and I did not have a good relationship. He took pride in his demeaning behavior toward me during my childhood.

Michal, P.W.'s wife, often criticized me for not having a good relationship with him, but she did not know about the sexual abuse I was exposed to as a child. I did not tell her until I graduated from University. When she asked why I did not tell her sooner I said I knew it would break up the family. I had already come from a broken family and did not want to be the reason for another family falling apart.

Many children blame themselves for the mistakes of their parents. This is one tool of deception that the enemy will use to cover their identity with condemnation. Having to carry the weight of their parents' mistakes is already enough for them without having to also identify with blame and shame due to thinking they are the reason for those same mistakes. This is why teaching children that they identify with Christ and His love is vital to their development and wellbeing.

CHAPTER SEVEN

Second Foster Home

**"Do you not know that your body is a temple of
the Holy Spirit who is within you, whom you
have [received as a gift] from God, and that you
are not your own [property]?"
1 Corinthians 6:19**

When I was in second grade, P.W. decided
they were incapable of caring for eight kids, so
Solomon, Samson, Orpah, and I all moved in
with another foster family. Who could blame
him really? Eight children are a lot, especially
since none were his own biological children.
Still, no one was aware of the sexual abuse that
had taken place.

God had His hand on our lives when He next
placed us with a pastor and his wife. They were
older, more like grandparents, but they were
sweet, and they took care of us. They were an
actual foster home who had fostered many
children over the years, but they were not
looking to adopt. We became super involved in
their church and I learned about Jesus through
their Awana program. I was a Sparky if you
know what that is.

We lived with the pastor and his wife for
eight months before Michal returned to load us

and all our belongings into her van and moved us all back to her house. Although my family life was not always the best, I had a good childhood. I grew up very religious, and rarely missed a church service. We were there every Sunday morning, Sunday night, and Wednesday night.

Religion

Both Michal and P.W. came from strict religious backgrounds. P.W.'s father was a pastor. We probably went to more than twenty different churches, because whenever they did not agree with the teachings of a church, we moved to another church. The root of religion is control, many man-made rules that do not always line up with the Bible. Some pastors actually use scripture to manipulate and control their congregations. It is far from godly and it pushes people away from having a true relationship with Jesus Christ. It is one thing to know *about* Jesus, but it is altogether different to actually know Him and to be known by Him.

People of the church can often be hypocritical, too, because of their religious views, but God never intended for us to be spectators. He calls us to be participants in the true Gospel that transforms us from the inside out. Transformation causes us to live holy as we hunger after God's presence in our lives, more than any program that focuses on the church's agenda rather than God's agenda. The true definition of Church is when you and I go outside the four walls of the building and allow God to use us as a holy demonstration of His great power flowing through us.

It is one thing to sit in church, but it is altogether different to BE Church by taking on the role of a disciple who exemplifies Christ, *"Heal the sick, raise the dead, cleanse the lepers, cast out demons. Freely you have received, freely give."* (Matt. 10:8)

God calls us to preach and teach about the love of Jesus everywhere we go, even in our everyday life. Someone who can turn Jesus on and off, based on the atmosphere and the people they hang around with, has not really encountered His true nature. When we have a true, authentic relationship with Jesus, we cannot help but tell others how blessed we are to know Him. The Word of God equips us in and out of season to share Him with others.

Never underestimate the power of a seed sown into a potential believer of Jesus Christ. We never know who God will bring into their life next, to water and nurture the same seed God had us plant out of obedience by yielding to His voice. That is why it is so important for each one of us to get out of our comfort zone and be who God has called us to be. We cannot let the fear of what others may think hold us back from telling them about Jesus Christ. Evangelism is just people sharing the love of Jesus and their testimony of what God has done to better their lives.

When you live and breathe Jesus and bear the fruit of love, those around you will see a difference in you. They will ask why you look, talk, and smell different from the rest of the people they know. Jesus did not fit in with the crowd and neither should true, consecrated Christians. Those who truly love God will stand out, *"That you may be blameless and innocent, children of God without blemish in the midst of a crooked and twisted generation, among whom you shine as lights in the world."* (Phil. 2:15)

The light of Christ shines forth in the darkness through those who love Him, and Christians separate themselves from anything that could potentially dim that light. Consecrated vessels do not listen to music or watch movies that contradict the truth of God's Word, nor do they hang out in bars and clubs. They are also careful of what they put into their temple (their body) because they are not their own.

Salvation

It is a true honor to write about Bro. A, the pastor God used to lead me to make the most important decision of my life. He is a genuine man of God who truly has the heart of the Father. He is one of the humblest men I have ever known, continually putting others before himself without thought or praise for himself, every single day. When I think of him, I am reminded of this scripture: *"Just as the Son of*

Man did not come to be served, but to serve, and to give his life as a ransom for many." (Matt. 20:28)

This wonderful man also became one of my foster parents. While living in his home, he took me with him to visit the elderly in the nursing homes. As he ministered, his daughter and I sang to cheer them up! It was he who first trained me in evangelism and ministry as we went from door to door, knocking and inviting people to come to church. Although I loved Jesus with all my heart, I was extremely timid and shy at the time.

I still remember the day when the Holy Spirit caused me to acknowledge I was a sinner and how He drew me into His love. One does not just become a Christian. There must first be an invitation only the Holy Spirit can offer. We cannot save ourselves. That is why we needed a Savior to come and die to take our sin away. It is living in deception to say, "Oh, I'll just say a quick prayer right before I die. That will get me into Heaven."

The sacrifice of Jesus granted us power over sin and the grave: *"But thanks be to God, Who gives us the victory [making us conquerors] through our Lord Jesus Christ."* (1 Cor. 15:57)

I was in a little country church, sitting halfway back, when I came to Jesus. Toward the end of the service I felt Him drawing me to walk up to the altar, repent of my sin and ask Jesus to come into my heart as the Lord of my life. Salvation and accepting the Lord into your heart

24

is something nearly impossible to explain, only experienced. It was as if an invisible string was pulling me to the altar, so I followed the leading of the Holy Spirit. My Wednesday night teacher was already at the altar when I arrived to pray with me and led me in the sinner's prayer. This was the day that I gave my heart to Christ.

It was a turning point in my life: God became my anchor in every storm I had walked through as a child, a teenager, as a young adult, and continues to lead me today. When I chose Jesus that day, He adopted me into His Kingdom. *"He predestined and lovingly planned for us to be adopted to Himself as [His own] children through Jesus Christ, in accordance with the kind intention and good pleasure of His will."* (Eph. 1:5)

Michal and P.W. adopted me when I was eleven, but Jesus adopted me at an even younger age, when I was just nine years old. If I had not chosen to accept Him that day, I am not certain who I would have become or what direction my life would have gone. Just like I do not know how life would have turned out if Michal and P.W. had not chosen to adopt me.

Jesus chooses us, and when we believe in our hearts and confess with our mouths that He is Lord, He adopts each one of us into His Kingdom. Physical adoption removes children from a destructive home and places them in a new home that protects them. A spiritual adoption transfers us from the Kingdom of Hell to the Kingdom of Heaven. God brings us out of our hurt and brokenness when we choose to accept His forgiveness and love. He brings us into restoration and healing, setting us free from every chain that had us bound.

As a little nine-year-old girl, I knew about God because I grew up in church. I was there every time the doors opened. But that day I went from knowing about Him to committing my life to Him. We can know about God and not be a Christian, don't forget the devil knows God and he quoted scripture to Jesus, but on that day I chose to not only love God, I also chose to follow and serve Him for the rest of my life. I must honor my denominational church background because it taught me how to read, pray and study the Bible.

And Jesus replied to him, "You shall love the Lord your God with all your heart, and with all your soul, and with all your mind. This is the first and greatest commandment."
Matthew 22:37-38

Outreach Center

Michal and P.W. became very involved with the youth in the church where I was saved and eventually became the Youth Pastors. They opened an outreach center for the church's growing youth group, as well as all the teenagers in our local community. This was a huge part of their lives as they spent every weekend at the outreach center, ministering to youth from all walks of life. Most were older than I was, but many stayed with us in our home where I watched Michal witness and minister to them, bringing them to the Lord throughout my childhood and young adult life. These youth still honor and respect how God used Michal and P.W. to help turn their lives around.

Michal and P.W. were under much pressure though! They now had six children in the home and three were teenagers. As they became more active Youth Pastors and spent countless hours coordinating the community outreach center, their marriage suffered. They were in counseling with the church pastor, Bro. A, who had led me to the Lord and later baptized me. Bro. A had a wife and five children, yet they agreed to open their home to take in my three siblings and me while Michal and P.W. worked on their marital issue

CHAPTER EIGHT

Third Foster Home

**"I will never [under any circumstances] desert
you [nor give you up nor leave you without
support, nor will I in any degree leave you
helpless], nor will I forsake or let you down or
relax My hold on you [assuredly not]."
Hebrews 13:5**

As I entered third grade my brothers and I
moved into the home of our pastor, Bro. A and his
wife, Miriam. Although our previous home-life was
not the best, I immediately sensed Miriam, our new
foster mom, showed favoritism toward their
biological children over the foster children. Their
daughter, one year older than me, was a rebellious
preteen who did 'bad' things then blamed them on
me. Therefore, although I loved and appreciated
Bro. A, I did not want to live in their home.

While sitting with Michal in church one Sunday
I said, "I am going to run away from my new foster
parents."

"No!" she exclaimed. "You can't do that!"

But I was being treated unfairly and determined
to get away from that house as quickly as possible. I
had my mind set on running away and even though
I had no clue where I was going, I suppose I needed
to warn someone beforehand.

One day when I did not go upstairs to eat lunch, Miriam came down to my room: "You know you're only here because Michal and P.W. didn't want you, Sabrina. They gave you all up!"

I have dealt with so much rejection throughout life. The fact that I have such a strong relationship with the Lord is a true act of God.

We had only lived with Bro. A and Miriam for a short time when my third-grade teacher sent a letter home. She felt I was not being challenged enough in her class, so she wanted to promote me to the fourth grade. All I needed was the signature of my foster parents, giving the school permission to move me ahead. Unfortunately, Miriam did not feel led to sign that letter. Her own daughter was already in fourth grade and she probably did not want competition between us. I felt so disappointed. Due to all the instability of my early life I had already fallen behind a grade by starting Kindergarten in South Dakota, then repeating it again in Alabama before moving back in with Mom before first grade.

Miriam's decision to withhold permission made me bitter for a few years before I forgave her for not allowing me to skip ahead to the proper grade for my age. Life isn't always fair, and I hated that I graduated high school in 2014. If only she had signed that letter, I would have graduated on time with others my age in 2013. I was not fond of the tassels and other graduation attire with my graduation year, 2014. I always felt a year behind. By the time I later graduated from University it was not as hurtful, but still … I often thought about how different my life would have been if I had been able to graduate a year earlier than I did.

But then I think about all the people I never would have met if I had entered University a year earlier. God does everything for a reason, and we do not always have to understand why. I am thankful that God remains constant no matter what. He never leaves or forsakes us.

CHAPTER NINE

Adopted

**"Although my father and my mother have
abandoned me,
yet the Lord will take me up [adopt me as His
child]."
Psalm 27:10**

Split Adoption: "Only One Road Away"

When I was eleven years old, social workers
in the state of Alabama decided some changes
needed to be made with my sibling group. They
brought Michal, P.W. and their four children
(Ananias, Judas, Abner, and Marah), along with
Bro. A, Miriam and their five children, into a
large room together with me and my three
siblings (Solomon, Samson, and Orpah) to watch
how we all interacted with one another. After a
few hours of observation their final decision was
to split my siblings and I into two different
families – our worst nightmare.

The two girls, Orpah and I, were officially
adopted by Michal and P.W. Although pleased,

Michal was surprised the state allowed me to move in with them. Orpah and I shared the same mother, but Orpah was her brother's child, her niece by blood, so her hopes and expectations were high to officially adopt her. I was icing on the cake and we were loved.

At the same time, Solomon and Samson were adopted by Bro. A and Miriam. At the young age of four, Samson was very confused. He did not want to be separated from Michal! He had lived with her for so much of his life he thought Michal was his biological mother. Can you imagine a child more traumatized by being separated from someone who had simply cared

for him, rather than from his own biological mother?

The split was very difficult on all of us, and we all hurt. Through the many moves and changes in our lives we did not always have our parents, but we always had each other. We loved one another. As the oldest, they depended on me to be their little mother, to protect them, even boss them around if necessary and help set boundaries. It hurt that we could not live together anymore.

After we were adopted into separate families, we all still attended the same church together - like one big dysfunctional family. This was great until jealousy set in between Michal and Miriam, which eventually meant we did not see each other at all. My younger brothers, so dearly loved, lived only one road away from us yet we had such little contact with them. This all made me very angry, which led to bitterness that took years to work through.

Then P.W. and Michal pulled both Marah and I out of our fifth-grade school year to homeschool us because Marah did not like going to school. Abner was later pulled out of school, as well. I had always loved school and learning new things, so I did not necessarily care for the environment of being homeschooled.

In the meantime, Michal and P.W. wanted to have a child of their own. When they discovered P.W. could not have children, they decided to go through with a private adoption. They brought home my new baby brother, Samaritan, right from the hospital where he was born.

With the addition of a new baby, Michal did not have time to homeschool us anymore, so private teachers were hired to come into our home. In all actuality, I was sometimes my only teacher and had to be very disciplined to study my schoolwork. I struggled with algebra, so whatever I could not work through on my own, I had to wait for P.W. to get home from work each night to ask for his help.

After a while, Michal made Marah and I care for baby Samaritan. Marah was responsible for changing his diapers and I was responsible for preparing his food and feeding him. Samaritan had great problems with reflux as a baby and often threw up all his food immediately after I fed him, leaving me to clean him up, as well. Marah and I shared the task of cleaning up his puke when he would throw up in his playpen during the night and all throughout the day. We went through so many playpens with him. On top of caring for a baby we had to clean the house too because Michal said cleaning counted as our home economics class.

One day I finally complained to Michal: "But it's like Samaritan is like mine and Marah's baby!" There were times when he called Marah mom.

When I said this Michal threw one of her many little immature fits. I did not always speak up as a kid, but every now and then I had to voice my own opinion.

When P.W. was offered a job in another part of Alabama, the move was difficult, but somehow easier since we had not been allowed to see Solomon and Samson who had lived so close to us. I wrote about how much I missed and loved my brothers in my journal as a kid and titled it "Only One Road Away".

After Michal and P.W. adopted us, we often traveled to different states to be in court while my mom and Nabal's parental rights were terminated for their additional three children, my two little biological sisters and a baby brother. During one of these many trips, I even learned about the University I would later attend, through someone I met at the courthouse.

Homeschool to High School

When we were ready for high school Marah, Abner, and I entered a prep school where uniforms were required. One day I wore khaki shorts to school without Michal knowing. They were within the dress code and passed the fingertip test in length, according to my naturally long fingernails. I will never forget the way Michal talked to me when I got off the bus that day, as though I had dressed like a stripper.

"Just what kind of attention are you trying to draw to yourself by wearing those shorts to school?"

I felt her words were so demeaning and confusing! I certainly did not get in any trouble at school for wearing the shorts. What I know

now but did not realize then … Michal said this because she was so extremely religious.

After our first year of high school, P.W. accepted another new job offer with higher pay and we moved from Alabama to Georgia. It meant Orpha and I were moving even further away from Solomon and Sampson and we only got to see them one last time. The difficult transition of beginning my sophomore year at a new high school in a different state was made easier by the friends we made at the new church we joined. The difference in school schedules meant we had an extra month off that summer, so the church youth came over to our house every weekend for a swim in our new pool and we loved it!

That fall I got a friend request on Facebook from Mark, my half-brother. I had only seen him one time, when Solomon was sick in the hospital, so I was excited to connect with him again. This is when I discovered his birthday is on January 24, 1995 and, with my birthday on March 25, 1995, we are basically twins. Now, we not only live in the same state, but the same county.

Halfway through my sophomore year Marah wanted to be homeschooled again, so Michal decided to pull us both out of school, and I was not happy about it. I still preferred to attend

school and loved learning but did not go back to
public school until we moved to another part of
Georgia. By then I was halfway through my
senior year. I had told Michal I may have trouble
getting into a university because I was
homeschooled, so she enrolled us both halfway
through the school year. I am so thankful that our
guidance counselor fixed my transcript so I
ended up graduating with honors. My English
teacher also wrote a letter of recommendation
that basically got me into college.

In the meantime, we started attending a strict
(cultish) denominational church that required all
females to wear long skirts in public. Since I am
only five feet tall, it was difficult for me to keep
myself from tripping any time I attempted to
walk up steps in a long skirt.

High School to University

When I got the phone call that I had been
accepted to my university of choice, I
immediately started packing my bags for a move
to Florida. Michal and P.W. were very shocked
when I told them I had been accepted to a private
university and they did not like my decision to
move so far away.

"The only reason you chose that university is

because it's on the beach!" Michal exclaimed. (I mean, can you blame me?)

"Well, you want me to be happy, don't you?" I replied.

CHAPTER TEN

University

"Honor (respect, obey, care for) your father and your mother, as the Lord your God has commanded you, so that your days [on the earth] may be prolonged and so that it may go well with you in the land which the Lord your God gives you."
Deuteronomy 5:16

Turning Point

I chose to attend a private Christian university to study Psychology from a Christian perspective. I did not want to study psychology at a secular university because the teaching may be weird since Freud, a founding psychologist, used a lot of drugs. A Bible class was required, and I was excited to share with Michal all I had been reading and learning from our studies on the Book of Revelation, but she immediately began to warn me to be careful of my professors' 'false teachings'. I was reading the book of Revelation on my own, no one was trying to teach me anything. This conversation was discouraging, but college was a huge turning point in my life.

I went through a "dry season" with the Lord my freshman year. Many college students, or anyone who moves away from their parents, go through a time where they begin to wonder if their relationship with the Lord is real. I did not have a car so I could only go to church when my friends went, but other than that it was just the Lord and me. The enemy tried to make me believe He had left me, but I quickly realized my relationship with the Lord was no longer associated with what my parents believed or how they raised me. Now it was all on me and I knew God was real. I also realized no one could make my decisions for me. I loved God. I continued to take my relationship with Him seriously and I refused to compromise.

This is why college was such a huge turning point for me spiritually.

I watched many of my friends and peers live a dry, gray-zone lifestyle, and tormented by the enemy as a result. Although I majored in Psychology, it was difficult to believe in the reality of anxiety and depression. I believe every diagnosis and sickness has a spiritual root, in addition to a biological one. So when I saw my friends tormented with these disorders, I could not help but think they had allowed something into their life that had opened some kind of door to the enemy that caused their suffering (like watching Harry Potter or listening to negative music).

Although I chose to attend a private Christian University, it did not take long to figure out most of the people there did not practice living for Jesus as I did. One weekend a few of us girls went on a trip and while we were eating lunch one day they started asking, "Why do you not curse, Sabrina?"

"I didn't grow up cursing, and I am not about to start now that I'm at university," I responded.

One said, "Oh, don't worry. You'll be cursing with the rest of us by the end of the year."

I never picked up on it, and I am now a university graduate. I came from a strict religious background, but it was more focused on control and manipulation than it was about being holy and maintaining a pure heart before the Lord. I grew up watching horror movies. Even though I did not enjoy them, I liked the adrenaline rush they gave. I later discovered my perspective was deceptive and allowed the enemy to fill me with fear.

One night while looking for something to do at some friends' dorm, they suggested we watch a movie. When I offered the title of a horror movie, they were shocked! I thought, "You guys don't see anything wrong with watching shows and movies with sexual content, but watching a horror movie is wrong?"

I saw absolutely nothing wrong with watching, what I considered, clean horror movies. I grew up in church, but no one had ever taught me about the spiritual realm or the consequences that may come from watching horror movies. This is why God tells us in the book of Hosea: *"People die from their lack of knowledge."* (Hos. 4:6)

It is so important to not just read the Bible but to digest it and apply it to our everyday lives.

I did not want to stand out from anyone, but wearing skirts all the time did just that, and the differences in lifestyles of my peers caused me to stand out even more.

One day a close friend asked, "Do you feel wearing skirts makes you better than the other girls? Nobody believes in wearing skirts all the time like you do."

This question bothered me and made me realize there were people I probably could not reach, simply because I wore a long skirt all the time. It also made me realize how much bondage I was under from the religious mindset of the church we attended when I was in high school, and how strict they were in making me conform to their rules. After much religious mental turmoil, the long skirts were stored in the back of my closet. I did not want anyone to think I thought I was better than them, when I knew I was not.

Year One and Done

After completing my first year of college, I moved back in with Michal and P.W. Michal was still trying to control me and made me feel guilty because Orpah cried every time I returned to college after a visit. Orpah dealt with trauma differently than I did. Michal often said she could not handle Orpah, when in reality Michal was the one causing most of her trauma through her choice of words and tone of voice.

When I moved back in, I started teaching Orpah and Samaritan since they were now being homeschooled. We are to honor our parents even when we do not agree with them: *"Honor (respect, obey, care for) your father and your mother, as the Lord your God has commanded you, so that your days [on the earth] may be prolonged and so that it may go well with you in the land which the Lord your God gives you."* (Deut. 5:16)

P.W. came alone to pick me up at university and as soon as we got back to the house, I knew Michal was upset: "You are never going back to that college! You can just go ahead and transfer all those credits to the community college near home." (I was twenty years old!)

Well, it would not work anyway. Since the Bible credits we earn at a Christian university do not transfer to a secular community college, it would mess up my transcript! I decided to continue my education online, since I knew I would soon turn twenty-one.

Michal accused me of 'being wild' at university even though I did nothing to cause their distrust. They simply assumed I was wild because they could not monitor my actions when I did not live under their roof. After my twenty-first birthday, Michal thought it would be a good idea for me to move in with Ananias, my adoptive brother, who was a rank E-5 Sergeant in the United States Marines, living on a military base.

CHAPTER ELEVEN

Military Base

"Be sober [well balanced and self-disciplined], be alert and cautious at all times. That enemy of yours, the devil, prowls around like a roaring lion [fiercely hungry], seeking someone to devour."
1 Peter 5:8

From an early age I witnessed the effects of both alcohol and drugs on my family plagued with major addictions. I saw domestic abuse directly linked to alcohol abuse and I have zero tolerance for it. I hate it. There are too many "what ifs" and no child of mine will ever open the refrigerator door to find alcohol sitting on the shelf.

At twenty-one years old I did not drink. I knew Ananias did drink alcohol and I wanted better for him, so we made an agreement. If we were to be roommates, there would be no alcohol in the house. He knew what he signed up for. The first day I walked through the door I said,

"Your senior drill instructor has arrived!"

He laughed, but he had been a drill instructor, and he knew I was serious. And things did change for a time.

I continued my online education, while also working two jobs to help cover house expenses. I found a nearby church and started singing in the choir, just as I had all my life. Ananias occasionally came with me; he even invited a date to join us one Sunday, and there were times she went to church with me without him. Whenever we went in his car, I evaluated his music to help make him more aware of the content he was listening to, words are seeds.

After a while Ananias slowly started bringing alcohol into the house again, breaking our original agreement. Maybe it started the weekend when some of his Marine friends spent the day with us at the beach. He ended up drinking heavily, unofficially designating me as the responsible driver. And it continued to be a problem. Whenever I found alcohol in the house, I poured it down the sink. If it was too difficult to open, it went straight to the trunk of my car for the nearest dumpster on my next drive to work. I even threw his friend's alcohol away after finding it in the house one day. (At least he said it was his friend's.)

He was not happy with me. "Sabrina! You can't just throw away alcohol and pour it down the drain! That's a big waste of money!"

"We had an agreement, Ananias," I reminded him. "You wasted money to buy it in the first place. I never would have moved in here if I knew you were going to start drinking again. You know how I feel about it."

While I was there Ananias was promoted to E-6 Staff Sergeant and decided he had to throw a party for his Marine buddies. He knew how I felt about it, but it happened, and alcohol was everywhere. It is probably no surprise that parties with a bunch of Marines do not end until someone passes out, so we were in for a long night. I was the only sober person in a house full of drunks and I hated it, especially the smell of alcohol that came wafting through my childhood memories.

I was twenty-one years old and I had never even tasted alcohol. During the party that night I picked up a Long Island Iced Tea, a mix of four hard liquors, and thought it smelled pretty good. My personality is very black and white, so it is best for me to abstain from anything that could possibly lead me to become addicted.

After the party I told Ananias I had to move out. I had no intention of drinking and did not want to be in an atmosphere that may tempt me into trying something I really did not want to become involved with. It was one of the best lessons God ever taught me: No matter how close we are to God or how many times we go to church each week, we are never above falling into temptation.

It is very important to evaluate the environment we live in and those we associate with. If a drug addict is trying to get clean, they should not associate with those who caused their addiction. Just as alcoholics should stay away from bars, even social drinkers, when they are trying to stay sober. To get sober and stay clean, extra precautions must be taken to keep from falling back into the same patterns that led to the addiction in the first place. The Bible does not say we will never be tempted. It says that when temptation comes, God will make a way of escape. *"And He will not let you be tempted beyond your ability [to resist], but along with the temptation He [has in the past and is now and] will [always] provide the way out as well, so that you will be able to endure it [without yielding, and will overcome temptation with joy]."* (1 Cor. 10:13)

I thought I was strong enough to be around a bunch of drinking Marines because I love Jesus and have no desire to drink or even taste it, but when I realized I actually do like the way some alcohol smells, I knew it could lead to trouble. If I continued to stay around alcohol, I could potentially fall into the temptation to drink which, most likely, would lead into trying other things.

Most addicts and alcoholics do not plan to become addicted, but the influence of others can impact us. This is why it is so important to guard our heart, mind, and emotions. Temptation is real and the devil is out roaming around, just waiting for the right moment to devour us: *"Be sober [well balanced and self-disciplined], be alert and cautious at all times. That enemy of yours, the devil, prowls around like a roaring lion [fiercely hungry], seeking someone to devour."* *(1 Pet. 5:8)*

Sin may feel pleasurable for the moment, but its deception can leave us feeling empty, even broken. We cannot let our flesh dominate our spirit or we will lose to temptation every time. Just as I learned I was not strong enough to stay in an environment surrounded by alcohol, our flesh is not strong enough to resist the devil without Jesus. We need Jesus to overcome temptation because our flesh desires the things of the world.

God tells us there is a war going on between flesh and spirit: *"For the sinful nature has its desire which is opposed to the Spirit, and the [desire of the] Spirit opposes the sinful nature; for these [two, the sinful nature and the Spirit] are in direct opposition to each other [continually in conflict], so that you [as believers] do not [always] do whatever [good things] you want to do."* (Gal. 5:17)

Most people want to do the right thing, but it takes the strength of Christ working through us to maintain good character. Good intentions are never enough to keep us from falling into temptation and addiction.

Where Do I Go From Here?

Praying to the Lord about my next move, my only request was a place where I could grow closer in my relationship with Him. We are as close to God as we desire to be. If we desire to be closer, designate a part of each day to make room to be in His presence.

Prayer is meant to be a dialogue not a monologue. We want to speak to God, and He wants us to hear from Him; we only need to ask Him to train our spiritual ears to hear His voice. He is always speaking, but do we know how to hear Him?

It is sad to admit I did not learn how to hear Jesus until I was in my twenties. I grew up in church, I loved Jesus and I prayed, but I did not know how to hear Him. The world is so loud with so many distractions, both positive and negative. Letting distractions keep us from God's presence, even if they are not harmful or sinful, means we are not prioritizing our lives correctly. God spoke to Elijah when he was in the cave, but it was not how Elijah expected to hear Him:

And behold, the LORD was passing by, and a great and powerful wind was tearing out the mountains and breaking the rocks in pieces before the LORD; but the LORD was not in the wind. And after the wind, [there was] an earthquake, but the LORD was not in the earthquake. After the earthquake, [there was] a fire, but the LORD was not in the fire; and after the fire, [there was] the sound of a gentle blowing. When Elijah heard the sound, he wrapped his face in his mantle (cloak) and went out and stood in the entrance of the cave. And behold, a voice came to him and said, "What are you doing here, Elijah?"

(1 Kings 19:11-13)

We must get away from all the noise and get quiet before the Lord if we desire to hear Him speak to us. God wants to be our number one priority, not just an afterthought before falling asleep or eating our food. Having a "relationship" with Christ is different than having a "religion" with Him. When we are in a relationship with someone, we talk to them and spend time together because we want to know them on a deeper level. So it is with God ... If God is our number one priority, we can know Him at a deeper level. I always say that we can never be close enough to God until we reach Heaven, so always strive to be closer.

After much prayer and reflection, I called Deborah, a friend who had invited me to share an apartment with her back in Florida, and asked if she still had room for me, but it was too late; her apartment was full. At church the next day I prayed that God would open some kind of door for me. I knew it was time to leave the dangerous environment of alcohol, parties, and Ananias's Marine friends.

When I came out of church, I found three missed calls from Deborah. Yesterday her apartment was full, but now a spot had opened, and it was mine for the taking. I asked her to email the lease so I could pray about it before signing.

I knew Michal would not approve, but after praying about it I signed the lease, and called to let her know I was moving back to Florida with Deborah. I knew it was God speaking when she said, "I think that's a good idea."

Ananias was not happy about it, of course, but I was excited to resign my jobs in Georgia, apply for work in Florida, pack all my belongings into my car and head back down to Florida.

CHAPTER TWELVE

Transition

"Do not look at his appearance or at the height of his stature, because I have rejected him. For the Lord sees not as man sees; for man looks at the outward appearance, but the Lord looks at the heart."
1 Samuel 16:7

Once settled in my new apartment in Florida, I started working with a family who had adopted three children with physical and mental disabilities. I was still taking classes online and eventually signed up to take an anatomy and physiology class on campus. I went into my new job position knowing it would be a challenge outside my comfort zone, but always believed if we are afraid of a challenge we will never grow to discover all the things God has for us to do in the world. This position was where I discovered my passion for serving others.

When God told Peter to step out of the boat, He did not ask him to step on dry, comfortable land. No. He asked Peter to step out of the boat and walk on water, right in the middle of a thunderstorm and raging seas! God was testing Peter's faith by challenging him to try something he had never done before. No one else on the boat was brave enough to step out on the water with him, but Peter's obedience to God strengthened the faith of all who stayed behind in the boat.

People are always watching and examining the way we live, just waiting for us to go outside of the ordinary and try something that questions their belief system. When the family I worked for asked if I wanted to join them on an all-expense-paid trip to Disney World with them, I was excited! We never know the opportunities and open doors we may miss when we refuse to be challenged.

The next day I bought four new pairs of shorts for the trip, being mindful of how modest and appropriate they were. I even bought a size larger to assure they were not tight or revealing. The trip was wonderful and when I returned an adoptive family member saw my picture on Facebook wearing my new shorts in Orlando. And guess what? Michal called. They were still wearing the long skirts at home and now she was questioning my decision to wear shorts, just as she had all those years ago in high school. By the end of our conversation I was livid! She tried to make me feel as if my heart was no longer pure just because I chose to wear shorts. Unlike Michal, God knows my heart. I did not feel wearing shorts made me less pure or holy.

I stood in front of the mirror that day studying the shorts I was wearing and feeling confused about why they were so wrong. Maybe if they were tight or revealing I could understand, but that was not the issue. Michal's religious idea bothered me and made me realize how religion sometimes causes people to judge the appearance of others in a way that does not line up with God's word: *"Do not look at his appearance or at the height of his stature, because I have rejected him. For the Lord sees not as man sees; for man looks at the outward appearance, but the Lord looks at the heart." (1 Sam. 16:7)*

A couple weeks later, Michal called again to let me know Marah had decided she wanted to wear shorts too, and it was all my fault because I am the eldest girl. I told Michal I was happy about Marah's decision and encouraged her to wear her new shorts. A few months later, all the girls in my family, including Michal, quit wearing long skirts and started wearing jeans and shorts.

I later wore my new shorts on a weekend visit to Georgia. I always try to stay true to myself no matter who I am around. I did not change my behavior or beliefs based on what everyone around me was doing at University, and I was the same person with my adoptive family as well. I sensed judgement from Michal the minute I sat beside her and she had much to say about the shorts I was wearing that day, all judgmental and negative.

Out of respect for Michal I wore Bermuda

shorts the next day. While sitting in the front seat of her car she looked over and said, "Go put on your shorter shorts." Does she mean the same shorts she had so many negative comments about yesterday? My facial expression probably revealed I thought her suggestion was crazy. After all she had said about my shorts the day before, and now she wants me to put them on again? I was like heck no; I won't be wearing those shorts until I leave this house.

It was in college when I realized that I could listen to Michal's opinions, but it was not wise to make my decisions based on what she thought. I called her and told her that I was thinking about cutting my hair to my shoulders when she said, "I do not think you should cut your hair like that, shorter hair will make your face look fat." That conversation made me expedite my hair appointment to cut my hair to my shoulders. The next time I saw Michal she went on and on about how my hair looked the best it had ever looked. What? That is not what you said before! I did not say a word to her about what she had previously said when I was contemplating cutting my hair. She was too wishy washy and judgmental. One minute she was against my decisions and the next minute full of encouragement toward those same decisions. I remembered the Bible warns against the double-minded, *"Being a double-minded man, unstable and restless in all his ways [in everything he thinks, feels, or decides]."* (James. 1:8)

Many months later Marah and I both were

wearing shorts when we visited Michal's mother. They had the nerve to say, "Sabrina, your shorts are shorter than Marah's shorts"

"I didn't know we were having a competition," I said. "But since we are, I will WIN!"

Dreams

God's voice is not limited. God speaks to His children in various ways: through His written Word, through other people, through nature, through an audible voice (I have yet to hear), through visions and dreams, just to name a few. God communicates with me in many different ways. One of those ways is through dreams, though it was not always this way. I went through a season where the enemy literally tormented me in my dreams before I discovered that the Lord could speak to me through my dreams. Hearing sermons on dreams and visions is extremely rare coming from a denominational church background as I did. Sermons on dreams and visions only applied to Biblical history that no longer had a place in today's teachings.

The Bible has numerous references where God spoke to His servants through dreams and visions in both the Old and New Testaments, and He continues to do so because God never changes: *"Jesus Christ is [eternally changeless, always] the same yesterday and today and forever." (Heb. 13:8)*

The devil always tries to attack our spiritual gifts, especially when we are unaware of them, and this is what happened to me. The devil tried to torture me through dreams where I was in demonic situations, trying to say, "Jesus." I saw myself trying to verbalize His name but heard nothing.

I also had dreams about other people that woke me up between 3:00 to 4:00 am. So, I prayed and asked the people I had dreamed about regarding their relationship with the Lord. One of the girls was married to an atheist. The torment did not stop at this. When I woke one morning and tried to lift my head, I realized I could not. I felt some kind of dark presence was holding me down.

This went on for several months, living in torment, almost to the point where I did not want to sleep at all. So I reached out to Michal, who suggested I talk to their pastor's wife for some advice. When I talked to her, she told me to look up John Ramirez and watch his testimony on YouTube.

This is when I realized our souls do not sleep at all and became aware of how important it is to guard what goes into it. I also had a revelation where God opened my eyes to the fact that there is no fear in Heaven, which led me to question why I would purposefully fill myself with fear on Earth by watching horror movies. After that, I never watched another horror movie again. When friends asked if I wanted to go see the latest horror movie at the movie theatre, I declined their offer. I even told my adoptive family that I quit watching horror movies.

Michal asked, "Are you going to stop riding roller coasters, too? That causes fear."

"It is not the same thing. Riding roller coasters is not demonic." (I am an adrenaline junkie.)

I was very careful with the words I used with my adoptive family because of their religious mindset. I never want to start unnecessary arguments. I always tried to be a peacemaker, but the closer I got to the Lord, the harder it was to maintain peace. They never agreed with what I believe; they cannot even "agree to disagree" without becoming judgmental, wanting to prove I am wrong. So, trying to maintain peace, I stopped telling them how I was growing with the Lord. I purposely did not tell them that I left my denominational church for a non-denominational church until a year later.

CHAPTER THIRTEEN

Ways The Lord Speaks To Us

"Trust in _and_ rely confidently on the Lord with all your heart. And do not rely on your own insight _or_ understanding. In all your ways know _and_ acknowledge _and_ recognize Him, And He will make your paths straight _and_ smooth [removing obstacles that block your way]."
Proverbs 3:5-6

I had been attending a new church since arriving in Florida, but it felt like something was missing. The people were nice, the sermons were enjoyable, but I was not sure I was where the Lord wanted me. When Deborah, my new roommate, invited me to visit a different church with her one Sunday I welcomed the opportunity. And right there, that morning, I heard the Lord speak to my heart. God wanted me to stop attending the denominational church I had been attending.

And so, at the age of twenty-two, I obeyed the voice of the Holy Spirit and left the only church background I had ever known. I now realized what the other church was missing: The presence of the Holy Spirit.

When God says to move, we move. Do not question God; just learn to step into the unknown with full faith and trust in Him to direct your life and future. Often, when we arrive at the place He is telling us to go, understanding will follow.

Transformed

After obeying the Holy Spirit to leave the denominational church, I walked into the non-denominational church Deborah had suggested we try and started attending on a regular basis, every Sunday morning and night, and most Wednesday nights, too. At the time I did not realize my obedience was positioning me to transition into the call of God for my life.

I loved their style of worship, but when I saw a man and a woman enter the platform after the music stopped that first Sunday I heard the enemy say, "What would your parents think if they knew you were sitting under a woman pastor?" They would be upset! I knew they would. But I am also a woman, so it really did not matter.

The words *preach* and *woman* were never used positively in the same sentence in any of the many churches I had attended growing up. It was okay for women to teach Sunday school, but they were forbidden to teach over any men; having a female preacher was unheard of. I also wondered how P.W. and Michal would feel about my future husband and I, both sitting under a woman pastor. I decided to cross that religious bridge when we came to it.

One Sunday I noticed Deborah writing a check to pay her tithes. Although I never discussed it with her, God used her obedience to tithe to convict me. I had never been a tither. Michal and P.W. tithed and they were financially blessed because of it, but they did not teach their children the importance of tithing. I began tithing 10 percent of my income to the church every month because I had read what the Bible said about giving and tithing:

"Bring all the tithes (the tenth) into the storehouse, so that there may be food in My house, and test Me now in this," says the LORD of hosts, "if I will not open for you the windows of heaven and pour out for you [so great] a blessing until there is no more room to receive it. Then I will rebuke the devourer (insects, plague) for your sake and he will not destroy the fruits of the ground, nor will your vine in the field drop its grapes [before harvest]," says the LORD of hosts."

Malachi 3:10-11

One particular church service changed my life. As the preacher taught on the Baptism of the Holy Spirit, I felt the Lord drawing me just as He had when I was nine years old. I felt the same pull now at twenty-two to walk up to the altar and ask them to pray for me to receive the

Baptism of the Holy Ghost. I asked God to fill me with His Spirit, the Holy Ghost and fire, while the ministers laid their hands on me and prayed in tongues: *"Then Peter and John laid their hands on them [one by one], and they received the Holy Spirit." (Acts 8:17)*

After we prayed together, they asked if I heard myself speaking in tongues. They said they heard me, but I told them no, I did not, even though I did hear myself speaking in an unknown language. Since it was so easy for me to receive this spiritual gift, the enemy tried to make me believe it could not be true. Surely I did not receive such an incredible gift. If you are like me and have to research everything at a deep level and desire to receive the spiritual gift of tongues as it is for the edification of the believer (1 Corinthians 14:2-5) I highly recommend you read *Seventy Reasons For Speaking In Tongues,* by Dr. Bill Hamon.

I am not an emotional girl, but I cried uncontrollably after leaving service that day. I had just received the Baptism of the Holy Spirit! Still, I did not believe I had received the gift of speaking in tongues until later, while visiting Michal and P.W. She had been babysitting and when I went to speak to the baby, I caught myself speaking in tongues, not English. Michal was in the same room when it happened but apparently did not hear me.

Fasting

After I was filled with the Holy Spirit, the Lord began to stir my spirit. I woke one morning to the Lord speaking to my heart, *"When you minister it will be by the power of the Holy Spirit."* I automatically got caught up on the word *minister* and asked the Lord why He said that, and He brought this verse to my mind: *"Not by might, nor by power, but by My Spirit." (Zech. 4:6)* I knew if I ever preached it would have to be God working through me because I was way too fearful and shy.

This is one reason why it was so difficult for me to hear God say the word *minister.* In university, I chose to take a public speaking course online instead of an actual classroom because I was terrified to stand in front of an audience to give a speech. I even stressed about recording my speeches on a webcam, even though I knew I could re-record until I was satisfied before submitting it. I just had a great fear of speaking in front of people.

Another reason it was hard to hear the word *minister* was because, where I came from, *minister* and *woman* did not belong in the same sentence. I was so desperate for the answers only the Lord could provide that I decided to fast for the first time in my life. Although I had never practiced fasting, nor had I been taught, I began a four-day water fast, only drinking water. I did not know how to fast, so I looked up preachers on YouTube to gain more knowledge.

I wanted to know if women are called into ministry and I did not care how long it took to hear from the Lord. I even became a bit dramatic: "If you do not answer me, Lord, I will just die from lack of food and go on to Heaven."

The Bible says there are some things that will not break without prayer and fasting: *"But this kind does not go out except by prayer and fasting" (Matt. 17:21).*

Prayer is powerful and when prayer is coupled with fasting, things start to shift on our behalf. When we are seeking answers, trying to break a stronghold, bad habit, or an addiction in life, try fasting. It will not move God, but it moves our flesh out of the way so we can hear God more clearly. Saying no to the flesh shows God how serious we are about our relationship with Him. Trust Him to bring breakthrough as we yield to His instruction for our lives.

The Lord will not release His fire and anointing in us until we become desperate before Him and allow the power of the Holy Spirit to flow through us. I strongly believe this.

So I started to extensively research my Bible, with a concordance and both the Greek and Hebrew dictionaries. I studied every church that the Apostle Paul sent letters to and I studied every female named in the Bible. On the fourth day of my fast, I felt peace in my spirit about the research I had done. The verse that confirmed women are called to minister the Gospel included the names of two females who had been ministering with Paul: *"Indeed, I ask you too, my true companion, to help these women [to keep on cooperating], for they have shared my struggle in the [cause of the] Gospel, together with Clement and the rest of my fellow workers, whose names are in the Book of Life." (Phil. 4:3)*

I realized Paul only told the women at the church of Ephesus to be silent due to the context of the time period they were living in, but Paul did not tell the women of the other six churches he wrote to be silent. This spoke to me.

I had been taught women were to be silent in the church, but God used the truth of His Word to destroy the religious argument against women preachers, as well as His personal message as I woke one morning: *"When you minister it will be by the power of the Holy Spirit."*

If you are a woman or a man who feels God has called you to preach, do not let a man-made religion cause you to be disobedient to pursue His call on your life. Your voice is powerful and your life (the good and the bad) is a unique testimony that God wants to use to set people free! Experiencing pain teaches us things that cannot be learned by reading books or even obtaining a college degree. There is nothing we will ever go through that God cannot use to help other people. *"As for you, you meant evil against me, but God meant it for good in order to bring about this present outcome, that many people would be kept alive [as they are this day]." (Gen. 50:20)*

One Sunday morning I woke to the Holy Spirit saying, *"When you walk through the valley of the shadow of death you will fear no evil."* I knew this to be a popular scripture from the Bible, so I immediately jumped out of bed and grabbed my Bible to look up the twenty-third chapter in the book of Psalms. I wanted to remember the entire reference.

Later at church they announced a woman minister had come all the way from Texas to minister to us that day. When she told us to turn to Psalms, chapter twenty-three, my jaw dropped. It was one day before my birthday and the Lord woke me up to read this same scripture. I did not know who this minister was, did not even know she was scheduled to speak, but I knew God wanted me to focus on what she had to say.

CHAPTER FOURTEEN

Shift in Direction

**"For we walk by faith, not by sight [living our
lives in a manner consistent with our   confident
belief in God's promises]."
2 Corinthians 5:7**

My plan was to go to graduate school after I
graduated to pursue a master's degree in mental
health counseling. Since graduate school requires
an internship, I looked for a new job position in
my career field to help me grow in experience. I
got a job interview at university, knowing they
would pay for a graduate degree if I worked for
them. Before the three-hour interview, I prayed
God would open the doors He wanted me to
walk through and, at the same time, close the
doors that would lead me in the wrong direction,
according to His will.

A few days later I learned the position had
gone to someone else. I already had another
interview lined up with a nearby psychiatric
hospital but on the way, a closed bridge
prompted me to return home. I felt it was a sure
sign to decline the position.

Shortly before graduation my desires for a
future career began to change. In all honesty this
freaked me out. I am the type of girl who likes to

cross all the t's, dot all the i's, and have my plans set in stone, but this is not how the Lord works.
I ended up changing the direction of my career from counseling, to neuropsychology, before accepting a full-time job in ministry with Noadiah, an evangelist, for whom I ultimately worked for nearly two years.

Israel

I met Noadiah on Easter Sunday in the Spring of my graduation from University. She invited me to several functions where we got to know each other better and offered me a job I could not accept until after I attended to several other prior commitments.

My original intent for knowing her was to be connected with an internship for grad school. She had previously graduated and received a masters degree in mental health counseling from my university. She told me when she first met me that I was so much like her and our meeting was divine. She also told me she had connections in the counseling field she could connect me with. When I would text her (she put her number in my phone) asking about her connections, she would invite me to her various functions. Upon my arrival her connections were nowhere in attendance.

The family I had been working for who had three adopted children took me with them to Universal Studios four or five times before I quit working for them. After our final trip together, I packed my suitcase to catch a plane to New York, with a connecting eleven-hour flight to Tel Aviv, Israel. I had the opportunity to tour Israel for two weeks and it was a life-changing experience. I want to go back! It is one thing to read the events in the Bible, but to have the opportunity to see the words on the pages come to life before your eyes is quite amazing.

One morning my roommate and I got up early to watch the sunrise and read our Bibles over the Sea of Galilee, where Jesus and Peter had walked on water. A girl approached us, and we somehow got on the topic of her back pain. My roommate suggested that we pray for her. As we were praying, I asked her permission to pray for her in tongues; I felt led to pray for her in this way and she agreed. We prayed for her and I prayed in tongues, asking God to heal her; it was the first time I ever prayed in tongues over someone else in public. After we prayed, I asked how her back felt and she said she could definitely feel a difference. She did not say she received a full healing, but her back pain had lessened. More important, she said our prayers had increased her faith to believe God could heal her completely!

That is what healing and miracles are all about: getting people to **believe** God for the miracle they need. It is not about us being able to heal people. We cannot do anything without first being filled with the power of God: *"That you may be filled up [throughout your being] to all* *the fullness of God [so that you may have the richest experience of God's presence in your lives, completely filled and flooded with God Himself]." (Eph. 3:19)*

We allow God's power to flow through us as He uses us to minister healing to others. Just as the young girl said our prayers had increased her faith in God's healing, my faith was also increased through the witness of God's amazing power and conviction over me to pray boldly over her pain. We nearly missed breakfast that morning as God worked His miracles through us on the Sea of Galilee ... A surreal experience that I will never forget!

CHAPTER FIFTEEN

New Job

"From everyone to whom much has been given, much will be required; and to whom they entrusted much, of him they will ask all the more."
Luke 12:48

Before going overseas, I worked a full week 'training' with Noadiah and on my return continued working in her ministry, but never received a paycheck. She asked me to join her ministry training school and as soon as I arrived there was a sign that said "Ministry." After class we met for lunch and I said, "If I had known this class revolved around ministry, I never would have agreed to be a part of it."

I was still trying to discern if God was calling me, a woman, to ministry. I continued to attend classes for the next eight months, still unsure if it was where God wanted me.

Noadiah hired me as her "Personal Assistant" and "Ministry Assistant". I joined with others on her staff to meet at her house every Monday and Wednesday morning to pray together and finalize the weekly agenda for her ministry. Noadiah was an evangelist, and as her Personal Assistant, I would accompany her on her travels, clean her house, shop for her groceries, take care of her dogs, and help Martha, her Office Assistant, with any office work she needed help with. I picked up and distributed donated food, and helped the children in her ministry with their homework on Monday through Thursday. I also taught them about Jesus twice a week. It was basically like teaching Sunday school each week.

When her Administrative Assistant quit a few months after I arrived, Noadiah said she wanted to give me a promotion, so she added all the Administrative Assistant's responsibilities to my plate as well. This included creating her schedules and travel itineraries, booking her flights, renting her cars, and arranging her hotel stays.

Then, on top of being her Personal Assistant, Ministry Assistant, and Administrative Assistant, I also became her Travel Assistant. She was an author so everywhere we went I carried her books, her purse, her luggage, and fetched her tea. She often complained about her back hurting and I wanted to lighten her load.

A few months later she added more roles to my responsibilities: now I was writing curriculum for the children and managing the administrative role of her ministry training school. Next, I was required to work with the youth every Friday night and, since she was a televangelist, I answered the office phones/prayer line every Wednesday night at 7:00 p.m., and every Saturday morning at 2:00 a.m. Later I also answered the phones every other Sunday morning at 6:00 a.m.

I have no regrets though. Many people gave
their lives to Christ and some were even
Baptized in the Holy Spirit over the telephone!

I was getting gas one night when a gentleman
I did not know stopped to tell me Jesus loves me.
I said, "Jesus loves you, too." And then he
brought up Noadiah's name. I was shocked he
even knew who she was.

"Be careful around Noadiah," he warned.
"She does not preach the whole Gospel."

I took it as an offense when he said this to me,
and defended my new boss and mentor. I thought
his remark was an attack against her because she
was a pastor, and I prayed to break the attack. I
never told Noadiah about it, but the next day I
did tell her Office Assistant, Martha. It really
disturbed me that someone would talk about
Noadiah in such a way.

Money Matters

I went to visit my adoptive family in Georgia
for Thanksgiving that year. Before I left,
Noadiah asked if I would care to come back to
help with her book signing at the mall on Black
Friday. It was optional, but I was always willing
to help. When I returned to Florida early, she
gave me a $250 check from her ministry. Aside
from paying for food when we traveled together,
and giving me $20's every now and then, she did
not pay much for all the work I did, so I was

very grateful for this extra 'bonus'.

Obviously, if I cared about the money I would have quit long ago. Working in ministry does not pay the best and I did not worry about it until I realized I could no longer pay my own bills. It caused so much stress as I fell further and further behind on my necessary living expenses, almost to the point I seriously considered quitting the ministry. I was conflicted and confused. Noadiah always told her staff that God would supply all our needs, and if we did not have enough money it was because we did not manage our money properly.

These financial worries caused me to press more heavily into prayer. Noadiah had convinced me that I was following God's will by being a part of her ministry so I had full trust in God. I was great at declaring scripture while waiting for God to come through and provide for my most basic needs.

After a few months, I decided to get a loan to pay all my outstanding bills. This caused me to fall even deeper in debt, which eventually led to the repossession of my car. (Lessons learned the hard way are usually the best, aren't they?)

That day I called Noadiah to say I could not come into work because I had lost my car and then I apologized for being so incompetent with my money. Noadiah played many different roles in my life (boss, mom, spiritual mom, mentor) and she responded by asking how much money I owe. Then she tried to turn it into a teachable moment. "I am not upset with you for being unable to pay your bills," she said. "I am upset that you did not come to me and tell me that you could not pay them."

When I told her I owed $1,500, she said her daughter, Candace, was already on her way to give me a ride to the office. Once there, Martha gave me a check for $1,500 and had me sign a paper stating the money was for working with the summer reading camp where we taught children to read. Ordinarily, employees on salary are not paid to work in the reading camps as it is "included in their salary". I knew this from working the program the previous summer, and a "misunderstanding" I had with Noadiah about something she had said to me before I started working for her that revolved around money.

After I got my car back, Noadiah asked to look at my finances which led to her discovering the loan I had taken out a few months prior. This information frustrated her to the point where she paid off that loan, as well. She also found out that I was so far behind on car payments, my car insurance had lapsed. So we went to Geico and she paid for six months of my car insurance. I was very grateful.

Then she asked to review my entire bank statement. When she discovered I had overdraft fees, she had us close out my bank account. Then we went to her bank institution and opened a new bank account for me with her name on it. We sat down together to evaluate my expenses versus my salary; this resulted in a $300 increase in my monthly salary. She said it was for answering the phones and working in outreach, but it was really because she found out my salary was not enough to cover all my expenses.

After all of this, every time we discussed my financial situation she would remind me that I made a lot of money, and then turn around to say I did not have any wiggle room in my budget. My annual income was $18,072, but since I now lived in her ministry house I was required to write her a check for $500 each month. After a few months of this, Noadiah said, "This is causing problems with my bank. Do not write that your check is for rent."

The next month I forgot and accidently wrote 'rent' on my $500 check. When I gave it to Noadiah she said, "I told you to leave what the check was for blank!"

I apologized and did as she asked: I quit writing what my check was for, leaving the memo line blank. Did she ask me to leave the memo line blank so she could claim my monthly $500 check on her taxes as a donation to her ministry?

Teacher or Deceiver?

One would think I would have figured out that I was being manipulated and controlled by this point, but at the same time Noadiah said, "You are so disciplined in your prayer life and eating. Now God wants to teach you how to be disciplined in your finances as well."

I went along with it. She was my spiritual

mentor; the one God was using to teach me how to be more responsible and disciplined. Since she had taken care of so much of my debt and brought me out from under the burden of financial pressure, I felt relieved and decided to stay with the ministry. I felt no reason to leave. What a blessing it was that God had used Noadiah to answer my prayer and take care of my bad financial situation!

A short time later she said if I agreed to assist her with her ministry training school, there would be no need to reimburse her for all the bills she had paid off for me. I thought it was a pretty good deal! So, in addition to all my other responsibilities and setting up to prepare for the revival services she hosted the first Friday and Saturday of each month, I started assisting her every third Saturday of the month for the next nine months.

One Saturday I loaded up my car with everything she requested to teach one of her classes: some of the books she had authored, some ministry banners, a stand for her tea and cough drops, snacks for the students, and other items. After driving thru to pick up her tea, I was finally on my way to set up everything for the class when Noadiah called.

"I'm here in the parking garage," she said. This was her way of letting me know she wanted my help to carry everything (including her tea) in from her car. I was caught off guard. I usually had the room set up for class by the time she arrived but that day, Noadiah had arrived an hour earlier than normal.

"I'm not there yet," I replied.

"Why are you not here?" she hatefully questioned. Before I even had a chance to respond, she angrily said, "Never mind! It doesn't matter why you're late. Just hurry up and get here!" Then abruptly hung up on me.

Next, I received her text message saying nothing had been set up yet. Of course not! I hadn't even arrived yet. How could it be set up when I had everything in my car?

Noadiah arrived early and was upset that I was not there yet. When I arrived and brought the first load of stuff up from my car, she walked over and said, "I do not like being mad at my baby. Can you forgive me? I got the time mixed up."

So I forgave her, no big deal. During class that day she shared with everyone how she arrived so early and then tried to turn her mistake into a teachable moment: "It just shows how prophetic people are always ahead of everybody else."

I did not have much down time. Because my work schedule was so demanding and my finances were so tight, I had to tell my friends I could not accompany them when they invited me to go places with them. This isolated me from everyone except those I worked with in the ministry. I spent most free time in prayer, seeking God's guidance through His Word. This prepared me to minister to the children and their parents in the two low-income/high-crime neighborhoods where I worked, with about fifty kids between both locations. These kids were not church kids and prayer was my number one go-to.

I knew I had many responsibilities but as Noadiah always said, "To whom much is given, much is required." Then she even started telling me when it was okay to talk to my adoptive family, and when not to talk to them. She presented it as another teachable moment - how I could set strong boundaries with them because of all of the brokenness and different beliefs they harbored. At the same time Noadiah crossed every single one of my own boundaries, yet I was oblivious to it.

I loved Noadiah and honored her with my whole heart. She was my role model, boss, mom, and spiritual mentor, and she said I was her armor-bearer and intercessor, even called me her daughter from the beginning. She was a very important part of my life and made me think I was following God's will by staying to work with her in her ministry for the rest of my life. She said if I ever left I would miss the call of God for my life and ministry.

I believed her. Not only did I submit under her authority, I also never said 'No'. I did anything she asked of me and I felt honored to do it.

And then … I started dreaming again. This time the dreams were prophetic. They gave me insight into Noadiah's ministry, as well as my adoptive family. I dreamed about some of the kids I worked with.

Noadiah taught me to pray when God gave me a dream. She insisted I tell her all about the dreams, especially if they pertained to her or her daughter, Candace, so she could interpret what God was trying to tell me. Since I was so new to the prophetic, I figured telling her was a wise thing to do. God began to give me many dreams about my life, about Noadiah and her ministry, and about other people who were also involved in her ministry.

CHAPTER SIXTEEN

Prophetic Perception

**"Pride goes before destruction, And a haughty
spirit before a fall."
Proverbs 16:18**

God gives us dreams so we can pray.
Sometimes He gives us dreams to reveal future
events so we can warn others. We must discern
whether or not our dreams are from God. We do
not want to make life-altering decisions or
accusations based on a dream without further
investigation into the insight.

God used dreams to speak to many people in
the Bible. He even used Daniel to interpret King
Nebuchadnezzar's dreams. And remember
Joseph's dream in Genesis 37?

*"Now Joseph dreamed a dream, and when he
told it to his brothers, they hated him even more.
He said to them, "Please listen to [the details of]
this dream which I have dreamed; we [brothers]
were binding sheaves [of grain stalks] in the
field, and lo, my sheaf [suddenly] got up and
stood upright and remained standing; and
behold, your sheaves stood all around my sheaf
and bowed down [in respect]." (Genesis 37:5-7)*

When Joseph shared this dream with his
brothers, who already hated him because he was

favored by their father, they hated him even more for telling them about his dream. This is why we must pray for God's help to properly discern which dreams to share and which dreams to keep to ourselves.

One night I had a major dream where God revealed that P.W. had some kind of mixture in his life, an infidelity. In my dream I saw myself organizing things into a box. I am a perfectionist who knows exactly where everything is, so I knew this to be true in the dream. After arranging the items in the box, I put it on the top shelf of a closet. Then I saw P.W. go to the closet and pull my box down from the shelf. When I next looked in the box, P.W. had mixed all the items up. "Why did you mix everything up in my box?" I asked in my dream, and then I woke up.

As soon as I woke, I began to pray just as Noadiah taught me. I asked God if this dream was from Him and, if so, what did it mean. I did not want to accuse P.W. of something that may be untrue, but I automatically felt the Lord was telling me that P.W. had some kind of infidelity in his life. So I prayed, if this was true, if P.W. really did have some infidelity in his life, God would expose it and make it known.

Shortly thereafter, God did expose the dream to be true. I had not told anyone about the dream except my brother, Solomon. So when Michal informed me she and P.W. were getting a divorce I was not surprised. It was actually a confirmation; God had already revealed his infidelity to me in the dream. When Michal began to describe what she had found out on her own, I told her of the dream.

"Why did you not tell me?" she asked.

I told her the truth: "I was not sure if the dream was from God, and I did not want to accuse P.W. of something if he did not do anything."

After this I started taking my dreams more seriously. I realized it was true: One way God speaks to me is through my dreams and the dreams kept on coming.

Disturbing Warnings

Shortly after I started working for Noadiah a dream had me in the driver's seat of my car and looking ahead, out the windshield of my car, someone was pointing a machine gun straight at my face. Clearly, I was their target. I do not believe I prayed about that dream; I was still learning God could speak through dreams.

One disturbing dream had me driving on the highway. I saw my car slow down and speed up, slow down and speed up again, and slow down a third time before another car crashed into the back end of my car. I awoke in prayer to break any potential attacks against me.

In another dream I saw myself put on a jacket before getting in the driver's seat of a semi-truck. I was uncontrollably driving this truck in reverse and no matter how much I tried to stop myself, the force was too powerful to stop. When I woke, I again prayed to break any potential attacks on me.

In one dream I saw Noadiah's personality flip to the point I became very frightened of this side of her that I had never expected to see. On awakening I immediately thought the devil had influenced this dream. Noadiah's character in this dream just did not match up with the person I had grown to respect, honor, and love.

One night I dreamed a woman was painting her vehicle with a gallon can of white paint. She used a paintbrush similar to one used to paint the inside of a house, not the body of a car. As she painted, she looked at me and said, "You can use the same paint to paint your vehicle if you want to." I woke with a very bad feeling - that was not the right way to paint a vehicle. It felt as if she was trying to do a quick-fix cover-up to make her car look more presentable on the outside. This scripture came to mind: *"Woe to you, [self-righteous] scribes and Pharisees, hypocrites! For you clean the outside of the cup and of the plate, but inside they are full of extortion and robbery and self-indulgence (unrestrained greed)." (Mat. 23:25)*

It seems I had many dreams about cars (which represent ministry). In my next dream Noadiah was sitting in the driver's seat of her vehicle while a woman in her ministry stood on the sidewalk reading a book. Noadiah started talking to her through the passenger side window, but the woman continued to read her book. Just then

Noadiah was preparing to drive off when all four of her tires fell off causing her car to stall out. When I told Noadiah about it she said, "This dream means my intercessors have been too distracted to pray for me as they should be praying for me."

I had a dream where I saw Noadiah driving her vehicle toward me. As she pulled closer, I noticed she was so tired she was almost lying down in her seat. Noadiah drove into a parking spot but forgot to put her vehicle in park, so it veered off to the side and hit a nearby vehicle, causing that car to hit the next in line, then the third car hit the fourth car, on and on down the line of parked cars, crashing one on top of the other like a string of dominos. Out of nowhere the sky turned gray as rain came pouring down from thick, dark clouds. (My first dream about weather). I was still watching the domino effect of cars hitting one after the other, when the last vehicle swiftly slid into my own car. Then I saw someone take stuff from Noadiah's unlocked vehicle and in the next instant saw the same person return the possessions to her car.

In the next scene of the same dream, Noadiah stood gazing into a mirror while I painted a messy white border around the mirror. Then she said, "Stop, Sabrina" and a beautiful white rose appeared.

"I'm hungry!" Noadiah exclaimed.

"Well, you've been through a traumatic experience," I responded. "People get hungry when they go through trauma."

I was quite shaken when I woke from this dream. I knew God was trying to give me some kind of insight. And so, I prayed. Then I prayed again and called Noadiah to tell her all that had happened in this dream.

Noadiah knew I received instruction and insight through my dreams. She even went so far as to warn me: "You must be careful, Sabrina. The enemy might try to use those dreams to confuse you about your relationship with me."

After she said that, I came to believe every negative dream about Noadiah was demonically influenced, whereas any positive dream about her was direct from God.

In reality, God was trying to warn me about Noadiah by revealing her true character in my dreams.

Desert Season

The first year I worked for Noadiah I dreamed I was walking through a dry, hot desert with no food or water. At the end there was a stand selling bottled water, but when I tried to purchase one, I realized I did not have enough change. This frustrated me, but to the left of us two wide doors opened to a room full of abundant, colorful fruit I could eat freely of.

Upon waking I wrote a note on my phone: "There is an abundance at the end of obedience in every trial" and included this scripture: *"If you are willing and obedient, You shall eat the best of the land." (Isa. 1:19)*

Before God can use us, He needs to know who He can trust. We earn His trust by allowing Him to test us. We make the testing process difficult when we believe others are deliberately trying to cause problems for us, or that our life is a series of unfortunate events. To have a fruitful life we must first adhere to the pruning process; to be purified and purged from our own desires and fleshly appetites before we can be used by God. Reformation happens in the wilderness, not on the platform. The platform brings pressure, and if we have not been consecrated in secret before stepping on the platform, the gifts God gave us cannot be performed to their fullest.

If we cannot manage our insecurities through prayer, we begin to seek the approval of others. The applause of the crowd becomes what motivates and fuels our ambition to do ministry. This is a dangerous place to be. If the crowd stops applauding the impurities of our character begin to contaminate our anointing, and sometimes we are not even aware.

Walking through fire purifies and cleanses us to receive a holy mandate from the throne room of God. If it is not holy, why would we want it? Recognition, status, wealth, and power. Serving "self" instead of God always leads to pride, and God has so little tolerance, He turns away from hearts overtaken by pride.

In the wilderness we are purged of pride, impatience, and jealousy. God uses difficult trials to test the very core of our hearts and transform our character to reflect His love. God uses tests to burn out every desire of the flesh so He can strengthen our spirit to be obedient to bring Him honor and glory.

The wilderness season transforms a selfish, prideful person into one who is holy and filled with humility derived from honor. To bypass the breaking process of the flesh, we use spiritual gifts that come without repentance in vain; character will expose the impurities of the heart. It is a challenging season to walk through, as it requires us to deny ourselves and be completely dependent on God. Obedience through this season is so crucial it determines how far we go in what God calls us to do for His glory. *"For the gifts and the calling of God are irrevocable [for He does not withdraw what He has given, nor does He change His mind about those to whom He gives His grace or to whom He sends His call]." (Rom. 11:29)*

Jesus was a servant before He was anything else, and His ministry grew out of His service to others. Spiritual pride (false humility) holds us back from where God wants to take us and keeps us from entering all that God has for our life and ministry. We are all called to work in ministry and wherever we are called, God gives us specific talents and gifts to be effective in our realm of ministry.

God calls us to minister in our everyday life through many different careers, vocations and the way we interact with one another. We minister in so many different ways - to classmates at school, others on our sport teams, co-workers, mothers and fathers minister to kids through loving care and discipline. Mechanics minister to us by their example of good and honest work. Nurses minister to us through calming our fears before drawing our blood and preparing us for a procedure. People who work in finance can turn around and give their time and attention in ministry to listen to an abused soul who needs to be heard and encouraged.

Some pastors were never meant to be pastors, maybe they were called to work in business. Likewise, some businesspeople were never meant to work in business - they were called to be pastors. We do not choose our own calling, God does. We mess it up when we try to be what we want to be instead of following God's plan for us. He creates and equips us with the exact skills we each need to be influential and successful for the Kingdom of Heaven. Joy is always found when we are obedient to stand where God calls us to make the greatest impact for His glory.

CHAPTER SEVENTEEN

Blinded by Deception

"Do not be so deceived and misled! Evil companionships (communion, associations) corrupt and deprave good manners and morals and character."
1 Corinthians 15:33

I treated Noadiah with honor and respect because, not only was she my boss, she was also my spiritual mentor. I never thought negatively of her because I honored the anointing on her life. If a dishonoring thought came up, I prayed for God to purify my heart. Everyone has flaws and those in leadership are not exempt. I was like a sponge every time I heard her speak and absorbed everything she said because I wanted to grow in wisdom and discernment.

During our staff prayer meetings Noadiah often told everyone there, "God has told me to keep Sabrina right under my wing because of the special call He has on her life."

I truly felt honored by God to be so close to work with her. I analyzed and observed how she ran her ministry because I knew God had called me to ministry, and I humbly came under her authority and leadership to serve and grow in the Lord.

"You are so much like me, Sabrina," she often said. "Your boldness, your passion, and your hunger for the things of God match mine. The way you discipline yourself to pray and study the Word is the way God designed you. God designed me the same way."

Noadiah's kindness and generosity blinded me to her manipulative and controlling ways. For one and one-half years, I worked for her, served her, and basically became her slave, all because I trusted her as my "spiritual mentor". I did not expect anything less and I was unable to detect her secret tactics of deception.

One morning she was bold enough to not only share a prophetic word that had been spoken over her in California at a prophetic conference, but she also twisted its interpretation. Anyone that was in that meeting that particular morning knows what I am about to say is true. Noadiah shared her prophecy with us, "I wish you would be hot or cold because I am about to spew you out of my mouth" (for those that are not familiar with this scripture it can be found in Revelation as it talks about how the Church of Laodicea was neither hot or cold for God). She tried to make her staff think that God was about to spew her out of His mouth based on how tired she had become from working in her ministry. Does this even make sense?

Her manipulations were very subtle at first, and difficult to recognize because she played so many different roles in my life. I did not think much about it when she controlled me at work because she was the boss and I needed her help to assure things were done her way, even if I did not always agree with her. And nothing was ever her fault.

When she discovered I wanted to pursue a degree in law, she convinced me I would be able to save money for college if I moved into her Ministry House for free and become the house mentor to the single mothers there. So I moved out of my apartment and into her Ministry House before she informed me she would pay all the utilities, so I only needed to pay her $500 a month. Noadiah had previously lived in that house for a long time and I knew the mortgage was already paid off. I later learned Noadiah was even going to make her own daughter pay rent if she wanted to live there. I never should have gone through with the move; I paid less rent at my old apartment. Paying $500 a month was not our original agreement, but now I needed a place to live.

After living there a few months, I asked Noadiah if Mary, a friend from school, could move in with me until she finished her law degree. Within days of her move though, Noadiah came over to apologize: "I'm sorry, Mary. When Sabrina asked if you could move into my Ministry House I said yes, but then Candace asked if I prayed about my decision first and I had to say no. I didn't pray about it. Now it just doesn't feel right that you're here. I'm sorry. You need to go." So within one week, Mary had moved in, then immediately moved out again.

Next, Noadiah told me I should be in bed by a certain time. This did not sit well with me. She even called to check up on me: "What time did you go to bed last night?" She was my spiritual mentor and I tried to honor her, but I had a hard time with anyone telling me, at twenty-four years of age, when I needed to be in bed.

The next thing I know, she sent a text: "Sabrina. Do not come to work without first drinking caffeine. There is something biological in your body that requires caffeine. This is not worth losing your job over." Now she was making caffeine an everyday job requirement. I should have quit working for her right then.

One day, after a staff member close to my age quit working for her ministry, she called me into her office. "You are my baby girl. It has been brought to my attention that she is posting things on her Instagram story that are dishonoring toward me. I do not want you to be influenced by the things she posted."

"I haven't been looking at her Instagram," I said.

"Good!" she replied. "Don't even look at it." Noadiah had a way of making me believe she was only trying to protect me and had my best interest at heart. Now that I am on the outside looking in, I can see all the ways she tried to control me.

One day, when I told her about the author of a book I had read, she said, "Oh! Don't read those books anymore." Since she was a spiritual mentor, I stopped reading any book by that author.

She took me to a meeting with her one time and as we were leaving, she said, "Always remember to ask me if I want you to take my picture before we leave any meeting. That's why I brought you along today … Just so you could take my picture."

Eventually I think she began to sense how I was feeling, especially since the expressions on my face usually gave it away. I spent every waking breath by her side, serving her and her ministry.

One day in the car she asked, "What is wrong with you?"

"I'm just frustrated with where I am."

"Well, how you are feeling is demonic, Sabrina!" she responded and ended up praying over me before we even got out of the car. I said nothing further at the time, but later told her daughter, Candace, how I was feeling in full detail. It felt as if my time serving her mother was almost over.

A week later, Noadiah took me with her on a trip. (I did not tell her I had no desire to go.) While on that trip, we went to an outlet mall where she bought me a very nice, expensive gift.

Was she trying to manipulate me with money? Quite possibly, but if I cared about money I wouldn't have chosen to lay down my life to work for her ministry. Noadiah was paying me on salary, but for all the hours, weekends, and trips I worked, it was barely minimum wage. I chose to work for her because I wanted to fulfill God's call for me, no matter the cost. If I wanted money, I would have gone on to graduate school after I graduated instead of choosing to join her ministry.

CHAPTER EIGHTEEN

Manipulation and Control

"Love endures with patience and serenity, love is
kind and thoughtful, and is not jealous or
envious; love does not brag and is not proud or
arrogant. It is not rude; it is not self-seeking, it is
not provoked [nor overly sensitive and easily
angered]."
1 Corinthians 13:4-5

Master manipulators and narcissists use
kindness and flattery to dig deep into our
vulnerabilities. They know it is much easier to
control someone after they establish a trusting
relationship by learning about what makes that
person who they are. They find their weaknesses
through seduction of the emotions and then they
slowly and methodically take control of the other
person's mind. If their manipulative tactics are
not detected early on, they become bolder in
taking full control until the victim's own life-
decisions revolve around whatever pleases the
manipulator, instead of themselves.

All too often we fall into the trap of allowing
people to manipulate and control us, which
opens the door for abuse. We want to believe the
person causing us pain is a good person, despite
how broken we have become. By simply trying

98

to please our abuser, we fall victim to a manipulator because we slowly lose who we are.

In my case, Noadiah constantly reiterated that God had brought me to a safe place (with her) where I could grow into all that He had called me to be. As I was cleaning her house one day she sadly said, "I always wanted to have three kids, but my husband left me."

Then sweetly said, "God told me this morning that you are my third daughter." She went on to explain that Candace (her biological daughter), her Office Assistant, and I were the three children given to her by God. Was she trying to fulfill an emotional need? I needed a mom and she wanted another daughter.

She got me to open up about my childhood, my family, my hopes and dreams, and then she used that knowledge to exert control over me. She expressed love and genuine concern for me, but it was always on her terms.

It is cruel, but a manipulator cares more about themselves than they will ever care about anyone else. A manipulator is selfish. If we ever do something they do not agree with, they try to take control of the situation to suit their own advantage. Relationships should have two sides where both people put in the effort and make sacrifices to maintain a healthy connection with one another. True genuine love is never selfish.

Always remember, a manipulator will pretend to be the victim thus making the other person look like the bad guy every single time. It is unlikely we willingly let those we do not trust have such power of control over us, but when someone we trust speaks into our life or tells us what to do, we believe they have our best interests at heart. Rarely do we see it as someone trying to exercise control over us, especially if they are involved in ministry.

God has given us a voice. Those who genuinely love us should care about our thoughts, opinions, feelings, and aspirations. People who only love the version of you that they have tried to create to please and benefit themselves are undeserving of everything we are capable of bringing to the table.

If you feel you have come under condescending authority or have been manipulated and controlled, pray this prayer:

Father, I take authority as a believer in Christ to shut every spiritual portal that I knowingly or unknowingly opened to the demonic realm right now in Jesus name. I bind the spirits of manipulation and control and I command these spirits to go back to Hell where they belong. I declare that I will no longer participate in demonic patterns and cycles of manipulation, deception, and control. Thank you, for setting me free from all bondage and restoring the Kingdom authority and identity to be who you have called me to be. God, I ask you to show me who everyone is. Show me the motive of their heart, intent, and purpose for their involvement in my life. Do not let me be

**deceived by who they claim to be. Show me
who they actually are. In Jesus name, Amen.**

Red Flags

When I first met Noadiah's daughter,
Candace, I discovered she had blocked both her
mom and Martha, the Office Assistant, from all
her social media and did not understand why.
Candace later moved out of her mother's house
without telling anyone where she went, not even
me. Noadiah warned me that if I acted like
Candace I would not be allowed to work for her
anymore. I did not understand Candace's attitude
toward her own mother, but now I can clearly
see that Candace knew a side of Noadiah that I
had not yet discovered.

She often asked, "Why do you have to carry
my mother's purse for her everywhere she goes?
She can carry her own purse!" It did not make
sense to me. I served and honored Noadiah out
of genuine respect and love. I was loyal to her
and trusted her as a mother and mentor. I did not
realize her goodness toward me was all due to
pure manipulation. Noadiah had me where she
wanted me and worked hard to pull Candace and
I apart.

I was a very close friend with Candace even
though Noadiah used it against me. If we stayed
out too late together Noadiah always had
something to say about it the next day: "You
know Candace isn't in full-time ministry like

you are, Sabrina. It doesn't matter how late she stays out, but you need to be mindful of coming home at a decent hour."

She often told me things in confidence, then said, "But don't tell Candace everything I tell you."

Noadiah did not need to remind me that many things we hear in ministry are confidential, but when it is outside of ministry and people try to be secretive and hide things from others, suspicion always rises against their character.

I was twenty-four years old when Noadiah said, "You're so much like me, Sabrina! I feel like you won't get married until later in life like I did."

Yet when Candace turned twenty-one, she said, "I think Candace should get married before you do."

Her opinion disturbed me and made me think about my future. This is when I began to realize if I continued to live this way, working 24/7, I would never have any time to date, much less get married. If I ever had any time to go out, I was much too exhausted to enjoy a life outside of work. Noadiah already controlled everything around me, from how many hours I must work, to who I communicated with, all the way down to managing my bank account. So naturally, I thought she would also try to control any future marriage and husband I may have.

"The best way to get to know someone is to work alongside them." She was trying to plant the idea that I should marry someone who worked in her ministry, but I had already observed how she controlled her Office Assistant who was married with a child.

I watched Noadiah make Martha (who was in her 30's) cry at a staff meeting one morning by the way she spoke to her. She probably saw my facial reaction because she immediately tried to cover up her domineering tone and choice of words: "I can always tell when Martha's getting sick because that's when she starts crying."

This is a prime example of how someone in authority can abuse others by playing on their emotions. This kind of behavior is classified as emotional abuse. If someone is emotionally unstable, they usually take the abuse by being subordinate to their abuser (I sought counseling after my departure from her ministry due to her psychological and emotional abuse). This also applies to marriage relationships and friendships, when one partner tries to control everything the other person says and does. Toxic relationships can sometimes be hard to define but ignoring the red flags can eventually lead to an abusive disaster, whether it is physical or emotional. Then the abuser just walks away leaving the other person sad, broken, and confused, trying to figure out what they themselves had done wrong. In reality their emotions have been played with all along. Manipulators get us to willingly play a game of deception before we even have a chance to realize what is going on.

I was overworked and exhausted from serving as her Administrative Assistant, Personal

Assistant, overseeing her Ministry House, answering the prayer-line, helping with the children in the neighborhood, picking up the donated food and so much more, even including full-time care of her dog.

Working for Noadiah's ministry slowly became my entire life. I was drained physically, mentally, emotionally, financially, and spiritually, and knew if I continued working for her it would do more harm than good. In trying to please, honor and serve Noadiah, I had lost who I was. Without realizing I was being manipulated, I did it all out of honor and respect.

It got to the point where I had no desire to do anything else. When I got off work I was totally exhausted, too tired to cook and, with no money to go out for food, I simply fell in bed to sleep as long as I could before rising to do it all again. I began to set my alarm for fifteen minutes before I was due to leave for work; sleep had become more important than breakfast. Every day I woke at 5:45 a.m. for a 6.00 a.m. conference call to pray for Noadiah and her ministry and half the time she didn't even bother to join us. Most mornings I applied my makeup while driving to pick up her tea order, before heading to her house for staff prayer.

Shortly before I left Noadiah's ministry, her manipulation and control went to a whole other level. I had developed a close friendship with Ruth, a longtime friend of Noadiah, and after church one Sunday I went to her house to do meal prep together. It was the New Year and I, like many, had made a resolution to eat healthier. While we worked Candace called me but I did not answer. Noadiah wanted me to attend a function with her that night, so after I was done at Ruth's house, I drove over to meet up with Noadiah, Candace, and Martha.

When I arrived, Noadiah started fussing: "I called Martha earlier and found out this is a formal event. Why didn't you add that little detail to my schedule, Sabrina?" (Remember, Noadiah did not have a schedule unless I created it for her.) As she fussed, my immediate thought process was, *If she found out this was a formal event, why didn't she let me know so I would have come dressed more appropriately?*

"Don't you remember me telling you to pick Candace up today at church this morning?"

"No," I said. "If you had told me to pick her up, I would have picked her up." I did not figure out why she was so hostile with me until the next morning.

CHAPTER NINETEEN

Deceitful Intentions

"By their fruit you will recognize them [that is, by their contrived doctrine and self-focus]. Do people pick grapes from thorn bushes or figs from thistles? Even so, every healthy tree bears good fruit, but the unhealthy tree bears bad fruit."
Matthew 7:16-17

On Monday and Wednesday every week we had prayer meetings at Noadiah's house, so after prayer the next morning she asked to speak privately with me in her kitchen.

"When I found out you were at Ruth's house yesterday all my alarms started going off," she said, and then ... "I do not want you driving to her house. I have known Ruth for thirty years, but she is not part of my inner circle and I just don't feel comfortable with you being at her house. Why were you even there?"

"I just went to her house to meal prep for the week," I responded.

"Well, you need to do your meal prep with someone else. You need to do your meal prep with Deborah."

I just wanted to laugh. I knew Deborah, my previous roommate, was not one to do meal prep.

"You don't need to be investing your time in a relationship with Ruth! You should invest in relationships with people like Candace, your friend Mary, and Deborah and her sister."

Mary was my friend from law school who Noadiah had kicked out of her Ministry House a few months ago. I was so confused.

"I just don't want you talking to Ruth at all unless it is within a group setting. You can text her once a week, if you must, but you do not need to keep talking to her all the time."

None of this was residing in my spirit. Now she is telling me who I can and cannot talk to. She said I should honor Nannie and Pa who lived in South Dakota, but I only need to call them every three months or so. I trusted and respected my mentor and grew very upset about

what she had to say about Ruth, who I also respected.

She then started walking around her kitchen demonstrating how Ruth acts. "Oh yes! Ruth acts all sweet, but then she will single you out and cut you off because she is all about herself."

As soon as Noadiah portrayed Ruth in such a way, I mentally flipped and realized Noadiah had just described her own self.

Always remember, nine times out of ten, when someone says something critical about another person, many times they are describing themselves. We tend to see our own flaws in other people, and this is why we are so bothered by their behavior.

She said, "I saw her trying to do this with Candace but I just prayed and God took care of it."

Then she said, "You don't need another mother."

I immediately caught on that she was jealous of the relationship I had with Ruth. The biggest shock about all this was, Ruth had a son that Noadiah had been trying to convince me to be interested in for months. And now she was trying to tell me not to develop a relationship with

his mother? It did not make sense.

"Let me take you out to eat so I can tell you more about why you shouldn't invest in a relationship with Ruth." Then she rolled her eyes, turned, and said, "I would not want Ruth to be my mother-in-law."

I was beginning to see Noadiah's true colors. She was using her authority to control me, while also contradicting herself about everything she had ever said about Ruth's son.

I had been ill with the flu when she said, "You know you're on the verge of an eating disorder, don't you? You're just not listening to me and when people get away, they fall into rebellion." I could barely keep up with her criticisms.

"You and Candace are like sisters, but you have become too emotionally dependent on her. She has changed her eating habits, and when we see our friends losing weight it's very easy to become competitive. Candace looks good, but I

already told her she is not to lose any
more weight."

By this point, I was ready to leave her house.
Candace and I were not in any kind of
competition with each other! Was Noadiah even
jealous of my relationship with Candace, her
own daughter? I was shocked at all she said. My
eyes were opened and my outlook of her
changed. I knew serving Noadiah and her
ministry was over.

While I was working in the office later that
day she asked if I wanted to go out to eat with
her that weekend, but I quickly said I already had
plans with friends. If she had a problem with me
spending time with Ruth, who was close to her
own age, why should I go out to eat with her just
to listen to her speak so negatively about her so-
called "friend"?

Then she said, "Well, if you find a little
window of time, let me know."

I was thinking: *There is no way I will be
finding any little window of time for you after
what you said about your friend.* I had no
intention of meeting up with her and no desire to
hear any more of her gossip.

In the meantime, Candace texted that Noadiah
had asked her if she wanted to assist her with her
ministry training school. I replied that she should
tell her mom she would do it since I had enough
to do as it was. It made me realize how
controlling Noadiah is. I had been her previous
class assistant, but this time Ruth was going
through the class again so maybe she did not

want me there to talk with Ruth. Noadiah literally used her role in leadership and authority to try her best to control my relationship with her "friend." I was thankful God allowed Candace to send me that text, because Noadiah never informed me of this decision at all.

The next weekend, as I pulled from the driveway of Noadiah's Ministry House to go to Deborah's apartment, I realized my windshield was cracked. A few months earlier, my car door handle was damaged by someone trying to break in. Seeing this crack on the windshield was another confirmation that it was time to leave.

When I arrived at Deborah's apartment and told her how I had slept twelve to thirteen hours every night that week she said, "Sabrina, I know you've been getting over the flu, but you have never slept that much. You are a night owl! What's wrong?"

"I think I'm on the verge of depression," I said, but immediately caught myself. "No!" I said, "I do not declare that over myself."

I normally never talked this way, but started telling Deborah and her sister how I felt about everything I had been going through. They had no idea! Up until this point I had kept Noadiah's confidences even though it caused much friction in our friendship. It had been difficult to hold those secrets in, along with all the hurt feelings that went with being under Noadiah's leadership.

Deborah and her sister had suspicions about Noadiah early on, but they were shocked to learn how deep it went. They agreed I needed to quit working for her ministry and separate myself from Noadiah as soon as possible. We ended up hanging out for the rest of the day, I even spent the night there in my old apartment.

I had no desire to go to church when I woke the next morning. I did not want to see Noadiah. Instead, Deborah and I watched Michael Todd online, *Transformation Church,* while her sister went to church. When Noadiah saw Deborah's sister at church she asked where I was, then invited her and Deborah to join her ministry training school. Noadiah had told me multiple times she thought Deborah and her sister should join her ministry school, but neither one of my friends felt led to join her ministry or her ministry training school.

Deborah's sister told her I was at home so Noadiah sent me a text: "I missed you at church today."

In the meantime, hearing Michael Todd's online sermon gave me even more confirmation that it was time to quit working for Noadiah. I knew it would not be easy. The ministry staff had become like family to me and I still consider Candace to be my little sister. So I was not only quitting my job, I was also departing from my new family.

I never expected to leave Noadiah or her ministry. She often told me, "God's will is dependent on you being a part of this ministry, Sabrina, so you have to stay under my wing to come into your full potential in God."

I was still new to the prophetic so I had no

problem believing what Noadiah, my trusted mentor, told me to be true. One time we had been talking about a television studio when she warned me not to miss the 'spiritual inheritance' God had for me.

I am here to tell you we do not have to worry about missing what God has for us. He established it long before we became aware of His plans for us. God loves us, and the gifts He puts within us will always make a way for us, while our obedience to do what He has called us to do secures our spiritual inheritance and any rewards that He has for us to receive.

The Last Prayer Meeting

After spending the weekend with friends, I went home that Sunday night and poured my heart out to God in prayer. I wanted to be honoring, but at the same time I was burdened by how I felt. While praying, I looked over to find a prayer card that had fallen on the floor. The scripture on that card brought so much comfort. The Word is a lifeline during a crisis as it renews our heart and mind with truth. I prayed as I read this scripture: *"For God [who is the source of their prophesying] is not a God of confusion and disorder but of peace and order." (1 Cor. 14:33)*

I thought about how everything on the outside of Noadiah's ministry looked picture perfect, but there was so much confusion in the "inner circle" due to narcissistic manipulation and control.

I fell asleep early but woke again at 3:00 a.m. with the immediate need to pray. The Lord told me I was being spiritually abused. I did not know what this meant, so I started doing research and found out that spiritual abuse is when a spiritual mentor abuses their authority. They replace the voice of the Holy Spirit with their own voice in the life of the person they are mentoring.

I was shocked by the reality of this in my own life, even though I still felt torn. I did not want to believe Noadiah would do such a thing to me. Then I felt the strong and immediate need to get out of Noadiah's Ministry House. I heard the Lord tell me in my spirit to **GET OUT** of that house. I then started praying until it was time to get ready to go to Noadiah's house for our weekly staff prayer meeting at 8:00 a.m.

On the way to her house that Monday morning, I heard the song on the car radio: *Burn the Ships*, by For King & Country, Word Entertainment, 2018. The Lord used this song to minister to me as I drove toward Noadiah's house. It speaks of burning old habits and starting new beginnings. I felt the Lord was telling me it was time to step into something new. This would require me to start a new chapter of life, thus closing the current one.

When I walked into Noadiah's house I felt sick to my stomach. I knew it was because I was discerning something, even though I did not know exactly what. We worshiped and sang for three hours and I ended up on my knees, trying not to throw up on her carpet which I could tell had recently been shampooed.

Now the weirdest part about that prayer meeting was that we never even prayed over her that day. Our normal staff prayer consisted of Noadiah in the middle of a circle formed by her five or six staff members as we prayed over and around her. We did this every Monday and Wednesday that I worked there unless she had a flight to catch. I had been working for her for nearly two years and in all that time we had never *not* prayed over her in the circle.

Weird? I know. She let us worship for three hours that morning, cutting into the time usually designated to pray over her alone. While we were singing, she acted paranoid and delusional and I could not figure out why. As we all prayed in tongues, it felt as if she kept waiting for something to break in the Spirit before we could transition from our worship into praying for her.

She finally turned off the music and told the staff to pray about certain things while she went to the bathroom. When she came back, she immediately stopped us from praying and told us to have a seat.

Then she said, "Sabrina, God wants to teach you longevity and consistency because you did not learn this from your childhood." This did not reside in my spirit. It actually made me uncomfortable. She started talking about spiritual pride and how we need to be humble. She told us that Martha was going to be with her as part of her ministry for the rest of her life. She had already told Candace about this the previous day.

For the first time since I arrived, I clearly saw the deception, manipulation, and control that I had willingly submitted to. After that weird three-hour prayer meeting (that did not involve prayer), she acted very odd. At 4:00 a.m. Noadiah had texted me a list of things she wanted me to do that day, but now she suddenly changed her mind and gave me her dry cleaning to drop off before I went into the office.

I am not sure how she knew what I was feeling that day, probably because she thought of me as her daughter. It was as if she could tell I was no longer spiritually blind to her ways. She seemed paranoid that I had caught on to what my spirit was detecting in her that day.

After dropping off her dry cleaning, I worked in the office until it was time to go do outreach in one of the neighborhoods where I worked. On the way, I stopped at a gas station to pick up some donated food and then arrived to help the kids with their homework. While I was feeding the kids, Noadiah texted: "You need to call me ASAP!"

We had a list of everyone who had requested more information about going through her ministry training school and I had been told to call about potential participation. Apparently, I had reached out to the wrong person. After I finished feeding the children, I gave Noadiah a call.

"I don't know how this happened!" she exclaimed. "This woman's name was not supposed to be on that list so now you need to call and apologize to her. Tell her you made a mistake! Tell her this meeting is only for those who have already graduated from the class."

This was a lie. I knew this woman had previously inquired about being part of her ministry training school, but Noadiah did not want to accept her. Why this decision was made is unknown to me, but it did not make sense. So this upcoming meeting was for everyone who had already gone through the class and graduated, and at the same time, it also was for anyone interested in applying to attend the next new class?

What happened at her house that morning was enough to confirm my departure from Noadiah and her ministry; now this was the very last straw. She had told me to lie to this woman! I was glad she was included in my calls! God used this experience to reveal another piece of bad character fruit in my spiritual mentor. The Bible clearly tells us that a good tree does not produce bad fruit, and a corrupt tree cannot produce good fruit.

I did not know why I had such a bad stomach ache at staff prayer that morning. Now that I think about it, my stomach also hurt at the prayer meeting in her house the very first day I began working for Noadiah. When I later told Deborah my stomach had been hurting all day she asked if I was nervous. Now I understand.

God always warns us before trouble comes, but God also gives us a free will. If we override His warnings, as often happens simply because we are not sensitive enough to His nudgings, we pay the consequences for not paying attention to Him. I learned this the hard way.

I did not grow up in the prophetic as a child, I learned about discernment when I opened my Bible and studied it. I never took preachers for their word until I read the scriptures for myself, kind of like a cross-examination. The Bible warns us about false prophets and tells us to test the spirits ... *We will know them by their fruit. (1 John 4:1)*

CHAPTER TWENTY

My Escape

**"Haughty *and* arrogant eyes and a proud heart,
The lamp of the wicked [their self-centered
pride], is sin [in the eyes of God]."
Proverbs 21:4**

I had a decision to make: Either follow my
discernment or try to ignore it. At this point the
enemy already had me overwhelmed by fear. I
was so webbed into Noadiah's ministry I felt no
trust toward anyone in Florida except Deborah,
but she was working until 7:00 p.m. that day. I
could not talk to Candace. She was raised by
Noadiah and, even though they argued often, she
was definitely under Noadiah's control. Fear of
the unknown was working so strong in me I
decided to stay away from the Ministry House
where I had been living. My eyes had been
opened to an entirely new side of Noadiah and I
did not know what to expect anymore. All my
trust in her was gone; I didn't even feel safe to be
around her.

Feeling safe and secure is vital to both our
physical and mental health. It is important to
know what triggers certain emotions, traumas,
and addictions so we will not be blindsided by
unexpected circumstances and situations that are

out of our control, such as the coronavirus. Never let yourself forget that nothing is out of God's control.

My fear drove me back to Deborah's apartment where I lived before Noadiah ever came into my life, and where I had stayed the previous weekend. I could not get inside the apartment until Deborah came home from work, but I still had the code to enter her gated community and having that gate helped me feel better protected that day.

I parked in the lot near Deborah's apartment, and immediately called Michal to tell her all about the manipulation and control Noadiah held over me. When I told her Noadiah even had my debit card and checkbook in her possession, Michal was shocked and angry, and wanted to come get me right away. I asked her to wait until I could talk to Deborah and her mom first. Deborah's mom is very discerning, and they could help me get a plan together before I left the state.

Having wise counsel when making major decisions is so important. *"And the person of understanding will acquire wise counsel and the skill [to steer his course wisely and lead others to the truth]." (Pro. 1:5)*

When Deborah came home from work we called her mom and the phone conversation confirmed my decision to escape from Noadiah. Picking up one's entire life to escape overnight is not an easy decision for anyone to make. My entire college life and young adult life was crumbling overnight, and although I had been through some difficult things in life, it was hard to process. I was losing my job, my work family, and moving far away from my friends.

I felt the manipulation and control were too strong to give a two weeks' notice, much less a day's notice, so the plan was to send an email stating my resignation the next morning. After establishing a firm plan, I called Michal and told her to come get me.

"I can't come for you now because I have to work in the morning, but I'll send Marah and her friend for you."

"I don't care who comes, just send someone. Get me out of here!"

While waiting for Marah to arrive we mapped out our next course of action. I needed to get whatever belongings I could from the Ministry House and leave Noadiah's keys somewhere. I also needed to withdraw all the money I had in the world from the bank account Noadiah had set up for me, remembering her absolute fit when I defiled her wishes by connecting a debit card to that account. I was ready to fly free, but first we had to get out from under Noadiah's authoritative commands.

Marah and her friend arrived in the pouring rain around 2:40 a.m. and they were ready for immediate action: "Come on. Let's go get your stuff!"

By the time we arrived at the Ministry House, I was in so much fear I didn't want to walk in the house. I didn't even want to take any of my things. I just wanted to get back in the car and go!

Marah said, "Come on. We brought our vehicle to help get all your stuff."

So I walked through the house and packed only the things I valued most. I was in a state of shock and panic to the point where I became frustrated with their help. I felt they were too relaxed and did not take the packing situation seriously.

Marah took a load to her car and, unaware she was still outside, I stopped dead in my tracks when I came downstairs with another loaded box and saw someone standing in the doorway. I thought it was Noadiah! My body was paralyzed with fear! When I realized it was Marah I started crying and we worked with even more urgency to get away. We were only at the house for an hour, but I was so frightened it felt like we were there for at least five hours.

Before all this happened, I never understood how anyone could just run away, leaving all their belongings behind. I was the house mentor of single moms and their children, and I had seen it happen time and again. But now I know. When we do not feel safe and secure, we do not care about material things. We can always buy more stuff, but we cannot buy peace. Peace is only maintained through a loving relationship with Jesus. We can have a false sense of peace by trying to fill our lives with everything other than Jesus, but it never lasts. Only the peace that comes from Jesus will last through a storm.

Noadiah had trusted me. I had keys to the Ministry House, her ministry office, even her own home, but I left all those keys behind, locked the door behind me, got in the car and quickly drove away. I knew Noadiah woke at 4:00 a.m. and often went to check her ministry mail at the post office. Her friend across the street also woke early, and I wanted to get out of the house and on the road quickly in case anyone decided to show up.

I got in the car with a quick prayer: "I am in no shape to get behind the wheel right now, Lord. I am exhausted and, in a panic, but I know you are going to help me drive away."

I had been awake since 3:00 a.m. the previous morning and now it was over twenty-four hours later. There had been that weird three-hour prayer meeting at Noadiah's house, I had taken her clothes to the dry cleaners, worked at the office, picked up donated food, helped the children with their homework and fed them, and then there was that call from Noadiah, wanting me to lie to the woman on the call list who wasn't supposed to receive my phone call. I had been dealing with all the confusion and convictions about my feelings toward Noadiah and the decision to leave. My mind was shot.

Now I grabbed my phone to block Noadiah, Martha, and Candace (whom I did not want to block). I knew just seeing their names pop up on my phone screen would be very traumatic in the midst of this final escape.

We had not been driving long when Marah

called from the other car to say, "You're in no shape to drive so we're pulling over in a few exits so I can drive your car and you can try to relax a bit."

After we switched seats I wrote Candace a goodbye message, but did not want to send it directly to her phone, possibly revealing my location, so I sent it to Deborah and asked her to forward it to Candace later in the day. I knew they would try to contact Deborah and Mary when they realized I was gone.

I was shocked, angry, confused, sad, and all the while had the full realization that my entire life had just shifted directions within a span of twenty-four hours.

The Truth Will Set You Free

When God revealed I was being spiritually abused, I had to act quickly on His revelation, even while adjusting to the news within myself. Completely oblivious, I had allowed Noadiah to dominate my life in the name of the Lord. When I realized I was responsible for letting her control me and hold me back from doing what God had called me to do, I made the difficult decision to leave, not only the ministerial authority I was under, but also the new family I had grown to love. I needed to get away despite what anyone may think or say about me. I had to leave what had become my comfort zone even though I was unsure what my future held. If God had not revealed Noadiah was spiritually abusing me, I never would have left.

One reason why we choose to follow Jesus is because He protects and guides us. Even when we do not know what the future holds, He speaks to us and points us in the right direction when we are obedient to follow His commands. When He shook me to reality, I made the difficult decision to remove myself from under the authority I had willingly accepted to follow. Now my destiny depended on my escape from the deception and dysfunction I was living in. I later had to repent for allowing Noadiah to become an idol in my life.

We are to ultimately follow God's authority and seek to hear His voice for ourselves. Prophecy and mentorship are great, but we must be careful who we let speak into our life. Prophetic words should confirm what God has already spoken to us. Those who let just anyone speak into their lives have not taken the time to develop a prayer life to hear God for themselves. They depend on others to tell them what God is saying, and this is a lazy and dangerous trap to fall into.

We can be confident that God wants to speak directly to us. He tells us to come before Him with confidence and boldness: *"Let us then fearlessly and confidently and boldly draw near to the throne of grace (the throne of God's unmerited favor to us sinners), that we may receive mercy [for our failures] and find grace to help in good time for every need [appropriate*

*help and well-timed help, coming just when we
need it]." (Heb. 4:16)*

When we willingly choose to let someone else
control or manipulate us, our complaints fall on
deaf ears. How we allow others to treat us is a
decision we can make on our own by raising our
standards to create healthy boundaries to stop
people from walking all over us.

God opened my eyes with His prophetic voice
by showing me Noadiah's heart motives and
selfish intentions to take over my life. She did
not change in her ways, but God's revelation
helped me change in my ways. It was my choice
to take His information and change the direction
my life was going. I knew if I stayed where I
was, God's true plans for me would be put on the
back burner. He would still love me, but if I
decided to stay under Noadiah's false authority I
would forfeit all the blessings and plans God had
for me.

The first commandment in the Bible is
"Thou shalt have no other gods before Me". Do
not let another person become a god in your life
just because you are too scared to stand up for
yourself. Toxic people who only want to use and
abuse us cause more harm than good and bring
damage to our identity. They play with our mind
and emotions until we think we are going crazy,
when actually it is the manipulator who needs
the help. We can draw a line to keep them from
holding us back from all God is calling us to be
and do with our life.

You are a precious child of God. He does not

want anyone to live under condescending authority, but He gives us free will to choose. It is our own decision whether we will please man or please God; it is impossible to have it both ways. Giving another person the power of control over us stands in the way of God's plans for our life and we become disobedient to His will.

We must be tough if we desire to do anything in ministry. We must ask God to develop within us a forgiving heart, no matter the offense against us. To be an effective servant leader, we must first learn how to forgive those who have hurt us because hurt and offense will come into every life.

CHAPTER TWENTY-ONE

A Cruel Betrayal

"This hope [this confident assurance] we have as an anchor of the soul [it cannot slip and it cannot break down under whatever pressure bears upon it]—a safe and steadfast hope that enters within the veil [of the heavenly temple, that most Holy Place in which the very presence of God dwells]."
Hebrews 6:19

When I arrived at Michal's home in Georgia, God was still at work directing my path. Michal had installed security cameras while going through the divorce from P.W., but God told me I was not suddenly safe just because I was now with Michal, not even with security cameras guarding the house. He also let me know the law would not be able to protect me, which was a little alarming. God said the only reason I was safe right then was due to the guardian angels all around me. I did not hear an audible voice, I heard these things in my thoughts, and I knew they were not my own. Both God and the devil can impress on our minds and thought process and trust me, the devil was trying hard to influence my thoughts as well. That is why it is so important to plead the blood of Jesus over our minds, *"And take the helmet of salvation, and the sword of the Spirit, which is the Word of God." (Eph. 6:17)*

By now I had been awake for over thirty hours. I tried to sleep but woke two hours later to find Martha and others from Noadiah's ministry had been blowing up my phone with Facebook messages and calls through the Messenger app: "Sabrina! Where are you? Please call! We've been praying for you all night long."

I realized they needed a letter of resignation, but I could not think straight, much less write a professional letter. I was emotionally, mentally, spiritually, and physically exhausted and still recovering from the flu, so I asked Deborah to help me write something. Within minutes she sent the letter, I proofread it, added where Noadiah could find all her keys, then sent my letter of resignation to her ministry email.

A few minutes later Deborah texted that Noadiah had sent the police to her work to question her about my whereabouts, then they called me on FaceTime a few minutes later.

"We got a report from Noadiah, your adoptive mother, that you've been abducted and robbed," one of the detectives explained. "She filed a missing person report on you in the state of Florida and we're concerned for your safety."

I tried to explain as best as I could, ending with. "I assure you, I am exhausted, but I am safe." Then turning the camera of my phone around I said, "But Noadiah is not my adoptive mother. Michal is."

Seeing I was safe with Michal, the police officially closed the case, then asked, "Do you want to open an investigation on Noadiah's ministry and the Ministry House?" I told them I did not feel capable of doing that at the time but wondered if they had received other complaints about her ministry.

To learn Noadiah had filed a missing person report and tried to claim me as her child was even more traumatizing. And she almost got away with it! We look so much alike we could easily pass as relatives.

When Noadiah helped clear my debt last year she had set up my bank account under her name. I had taken all my money from the bank during the escape, including my savings which totaled a little over $700. I called the bank a few days after arriving at Michal's and gave them my account number, but they could not find the account. When I told them someone had filed a false missing person report on me, she asked for my social security number. With that she was able to pull up a second account with a $0 balance, an account I was not even aware existed. Noadiah had switched the bank accounts around locking me out of my own account, which she had the authority to do since it was under her name.

I had been in a narcissistic, emotionally abusive, controlling, manipulative relationship for nearly two years with a boss who claimed to know what was best for my life and relationships, it almost resembled a controlling marriage. Now she had even cancelled my last automatic donation to her ministry and returned the money to me.

By then, I was in complete turmoil. Ordinarily I am not an emotional person, but my reaction to all the trauma caused me to cry uncontrollably. I had literally uprooted my entire life and moved to another state overnight. I was grieving my connection with the kids I worked with in ministry, many of whom called me mom, and heartbroken I would never see them again or even get to say goodbye. Still, I could not understand why I was crying so much when I had never been one to express emotion so openly. Later I discovered I had gone through every mental state on the feelings-wheel, and through more fear than I had ever experienced in my life. Fear of Noadiah, as well as fear about public opinions of me. She had called everyone connected to her ministry and everyone else I knew with a common theme: "Sabrina needs professional help ASAP! I hope she gets the right medication she needs because she is delusional and paranoid."

But more than anything else, I was in holy, reverential fear of God. I knew He did not want me to say or do anything to tear down Noadiah's ministry. The detectives who had worked the missing persons case were still calling for permission to open an investigation into her ministry, and this did not help matters. I knew my issues with Noadiah were on a personal level and had nothing to do with her ministry, so I prayed for God's help to be wise with my words and strong in my determination to say nothing negative against Noadiah or her ministry.

I called a few pastors to ask for prayer and carried my cell phone with me everywhere I went for the security it gave me to call 911, if needed. More than any other time in my life, my mind was in a desperately vulnerable state. As the days passed there at Michal's house everything felt utterly excruciating. I was exhausted, my guard was down due to fear and PTSD-like symptoms, and I constantly felt exposed to external attack.

Michal was worried. She suspiciously videotaped me, so weakened by exhaustion I could no longer bathe properly or even brush my teeth. After three days she started screaming at me, saying everything that happened with Noadiah and her ministry was all my own fault. My fault!! I was used to her usual screaming but could not take her loud accusations anymore. Then suddenly, I started praying in tongues out loud.

When Michal heard me praying in tongues, she called her pastor. Soon, two new policemen showed up at the house to talk to me, and her raving continued: "She needs to be checked out in a hospital! She's acting like a witch! She's trying to cast a spell over me!"

I felt so betrayed. Michal had never heard me speak in tongues, but it never would have happened if she had not used such a harsh voice to blame me for the situation with Noadiah. The one person I trusted most, the one I had come to when I needed help, just kept screaming at me until I just wanted to leave the house and run away. Her level of disrespect when I was already traumatized, added more fuel to an already raging fire.

After an hour of chaos and confusion, including my attempt to cast out demons, and Michal withholding my shoes and keys from me, the police told Michal I was just tired, needed rest, and finally allowed me to leave. There was no way I could sleep there anymore, even with my early-morning attempt to call and ask for prayer from trusted intercessors.

I got in my car, still cram-packed from my Florida escape, and headed to Chick-fil-A. Although I felt no desire to eat, I knew what I needed most was food and rest. I got my order and checked into a secure hotel, with keycard-operated elevators and a parking garage to hide my car. I was still scared though, remembering Noadiah talking about car trackers with a single mom a few days prior. Who knows? She could have put a tracker on my car the day before I escaped!

While searching for clothes in the car to take upstairs, prayer cards with scriptures especially insightful for my current situation kept turning up and as I read each card, I felt the comfort of the Spirit surround me. In the room, I had enough strength to take a shower and drink one liter of Fiji Water from the hotel room stock. I felt better, but still could not sleep. I tried

Melatonin, but that did not work, not even a second dose. Nothing helped. Fear can cause insomnia if it is not properly managed. I was too afraid to sleep yet running on ninety-six sleepless hours put me in a discombobulated state of mind.

I kept remembering that hour of confusion back at Michal's house and had the sudden realization that Noadiah had never practiced deliverance in the two years I served alongside her in ministry, even though she always claimed so many were saved, delivered, and healed under her spiritual leadership.

I also realized my lack of sleep caused me to say things I never would have said if I was not in a complete state of shock, fear, and paranoia. I had always been a closed book before this traumatic experience and never shared details of my personal life. Even Deborah, my best friend, knew nothing of what I had been going through until three days before I escaped.

Much later, I researched what lack of sleep will do to the human body and discovered, according to the CDC, twenty-four hours without sleep correlates with a blood alcohol content of 0.10 percent. I had never tasted alcohol or smoked a cigarette, so this was a wild ordeal for me, and one I never wish to experience again.

The enemy uses fear to mess us up. This is why it is so important to be anchored in the presence of God, especially when life flips upside down. We cannot always control what happens, but our reactions to what is said and done to us is entirely our choice. The Bible says a righteous man falls seven times, but he always gets back up with God's strength empowering him to stand again. We are not strong enough to endure shock, pain, fear, paranoia, and trauma on our own. It is important to focus on Jesus, especially when our faith is tested.

Later that day Judas, my adoptive brother, called wanting to meet up. I was close to where he lived, but I was afraid Michal had been talking to him, trying to locate me, so I turned him down. Being so sleep-deprived makes one feel as if their entire life is at stake. Logical thinking shuts down and forces us to rationalize with our scattered emotions.

I finally slept a bit and when Judas called again to say he just dreamed that we had met up together, I told him I would pray about it. I called a friend who prayed with me on the phone, then let Judas know I decided to stop by his house for a quick visit on the way to my next destination. I had a plan.

False Accusations

For some reason, I was afraid to go to Judas' house without someone knowing my location, so I called someone that I had become acquainted with through Noadiah's ministry, told them where I was going, and asked them to call me back. Why I needed a call-back was baffling, but I was not going to show up at Judas's house until they called me back.

When they did, I finally headed out, two hours behind schedule. Only later did I learn the only reason that person called me in the first place was because Judas had asked them to get in contact with me.

On the way to Judas' house, I received a text saying the police were told I had a loaded gun. I did not have a loaded gun.

But wait! ... That's when I remembered I DID have the gun Michal and P.W. had purchased for my safety, but registered in P.W.'s name. I had forgotten about it, buried there under all my belongings in the car. I had a gun, but it was not loaded, nor had it ever been. I never had any ammunition.

My mind was wild with worry and going all over the place. I had grown up with Ananias and Abner who had both joined the Marines, and always joked about taking me to the recruiting office for enlistment. I was ten years old the first time I shot a BB gun. At fourteen, I bruised my shoulder from the kickback of a shotgun. I do believe in the second amendment and I know how to shoot a gun, but it would never be in my nature to point it at anyone unless my own life was in danger.

After I pulled into the parking lot of Judas' new apartment, I called to see which one was his. I had never been there before, so he came outside to guide me. As soon as I walked through the front door of his apartment three cops were there waiting for me: two in front and one behind the front door. Believing I had a loaded gun, they were all paralyzed with fear; seven more police were hiding around the corner in case they needed backup.

They immediately grabbed me to pat me down, then locked handcuffs around my wrists and said, "You are not under arrest, just detained. Do you have a loaded gun on you?"

"No," I informed them, "but I do have an unloaded gun somewhere in my car." They were shocked at how well I was cooperating.

"Can we go find it?"

"Sure, but you really need to search for it," I answered. "My car is packed with all my stuff." I literally had my entire closet in the trunk and back seat from my quick escape out of Florida. While one cop was checking my vitals, the other two went outside with Judas to search for the gun in my car.

"Thank you for taking my vitals. I probably need it since I'm just getting over the flu." He asked the usual questions: How much water had I drank in the last twenty-four hours, when was the last time I ate, etc. He was surprised I knew exactly how much water … "One liter of Fiji Water from the hotel room last night." The policeman walked me out to his car in handcuffs and asked if I was going to try to run.

"No!" I said, but I was thinking: *Even if I did run, surely these big strong cops could catch a five-foot tall woman.*

As we drove away the policeman continued asking all kinds of questions: "Where did you go to college? What did you study?"

I answered each one, then asked the only question at the top of my mind: "Where are you taking me?"

"Your family is worried about you," he replied. "So we're just going to get you checked out and if everything's fine, you're free to leave and be on your way."

I had no idea that someone had gone to court to accuse me of having a loaded gun, saying I was homicidal against Judas. Which was more than enough to file an involuntary commitment to put me in a psychiatric hospital.

CHAPTER TWENTY-TWO

Forced Psychiatric Care

**"Because if you acknowledge and confess with
your mouth that Jesus is Lord [recognizing His
power, authority, and majesty as God], and
believe in your heart that God raised Him from
the dead, you will be saved"
Romans 10:9**

Assessment

I was involuntarily committed for a
psychiatric assessment because a member of my
adoptive family had lied, saying I was homicidal,
with a loaded gun in my possession. When we
arrived at the assessment unit, the cop checked
me in and stayed with me while the mental
health tech asked intake questions before
showing me to the waiting room. At the time, I
did not realize I was under camera as well as
police surveillance. I was bored and began
talking to a young teen waiting in the same
room, who had been there many times before.

He said his mother had locked him out of the
house because of his rebellious attitude, and I
took the opportunity to minister to him: "Your
home life will not change until you change your

own attitude, but God loves you very much. Do you want to accept Jesus into your heart?"

When he said yes, we began to pray. This young man asked the Lord to forgive him and come into his heart while we sat there together in a psychiatric assessment unit waiting room.

I was so excited that when a worker came to talk with us, I asked him if he was a Christian, too, and he said he was. I quoted scripture to him and asked where he was from. When he said he is from Nigeria, Africa, I no longer cared about where I was. I suddenly realized I had just been placed in the middle of a mission field with many different nationalities. So I decided to walk around and evangelize to whoever I could find. I knew they all probably needed to be encouraged and loved. I asked all the patients if they knew Jesus, and also asked the staff. I even tried to ask the police officer watching from the hallway, but he stopped me.

To be an effective minister, we must learn to respect the boundaries other people set for themselves. God is the definition of love and we must minister from a place of love. This is why it is so important to seek healing from our own brokenness and trauma first before trying to minister to anyone else. So many overstep their boundaries when it comes to evangelizing. We want to minister in whatever way we think is right without listening to the needs of the other person. We are called to spread the truth of the Gospel, but if sharing Jesus leads to an argument, we have overstepped their bounds.

There are four types of people: passive, aggressive, passive-aggressive, and assertive.

Passive people do not always have healthy boundaries, so when we talk with them about Jesus, they let us talk even if they feel uncomfortable.

Aggressive people often become argumentative. We can always pray for them, but we must be sensitive to their boundaries while speaking with them and step away when we sense they do not want to hear any more of what we have to say. We can still be bold and persistent in our witness but be aware and alert to respect the boundaries of others. Many people with this communication style have been deeply wounded by life.

Jesus came as a perfect gentleman, but those in His time who still lived by the laws of the Old Testament were offended by the truth He spoke. Yet even though Jesus stirred up the religious elders and priests, He never provoked them.

The third type is passive-aggressive. These people resemble those who are passive, except they act out their anger in indirect ways. They communicate their displeasure by using the silent treatment or speaking about others behind their back. Their words usually do not align with their actions.

The fourth type of people are assertive. The Assertives are bold and persistent and must take care that their boldness does not cause them to become bullies, so they do not overpower the conversation and cross the boundaries of others in their witness.

I have an assertive personality, so I have had to learn how to hold onto my thoughts, to keep from interrupting the other person. Think about how you feel to be interrupted by someone mid-sentence? When this happens to me, I tend to feel they are more concerned with their own opinion and do not care about what anyone else has to say. It is never our intention to make anyone feel disrespected or unimportant. Learn to speak with authority, boldness, and compassion. Learn to do this without being intrusive, interruptive, or rude.

I went on to minister and quote scripture to other patients there in the facility. It is important to quote scripture when we minister to others because it cuts deep and the Bible tells us the Word never returns void: *"For the word of God is living and active and full of power [making it operative, energizing, and effective]. It is sharper than any two-edged sword, penetrating as far as the division of the soul and spirit [the completeness of a person], and of both joints and marrow [the deepest parts of our nature], exposing and judging the very thoughts and intentions of the heart." (Heb. 4:12)*

In the meantime, I met with the RN who said the only thing she could find wrong was the bad cough I still had because of the flu.

"Let me make a call to your family and I'll get back with you."

I already knew I would be staying the night there. Sure enough, as soon as she hung up the phone with my family, she showed me to a room with a bed: "You can lay down here if you want to."

I had only slept a few hours in five days, but there in the psychiatric building I finally felt safe, secure, and secluded. My only fear was the crazy people who may try to enter my room while I slept but, knowing the staff checked in on us often, I closed the door, laid down, and tried to sleep.

I woke at 3:00 a.m., and asked for a toothbrush, toothpaste, and a hairbrush. For the first time in four days I brushed my teeth and combed a knot from my hair. And then fell right back to sleep.

The next morning, the doctor said I would soon be transferred to a hospital they had arranged. Someone brought breakfast, but one look at that food was enough to decide I was not hungry. I have no idea what was on the menu that morning, but it did not look appetizing. The grape juice was good though.

Later, as they prepared transportation from the assessment unit to the psychiatric hospital in an unmarked police car, the officer asked if it was okay to put the handcuffs back on. "Sure," I said, without the fight they probably expected.

I was not only handcuffed, but also chained. A device known as a black box was attached to the handcuffs, then a chain was wrapped around my waist and locked back into the black box, pulling my handcuffed wrists tight to my body. They helped me into the police car where a glass

petition separated me from another patient going
to the same place and, after a quiet twenty-five-
minute ride, we arrived at the hospital where I
would be involuntarily committed for the next
ten days.

Psychiatric Hospital

At the psychiatric hospital they removed the
chains and showed me and the woman who
drove the police car to another waiting room. By
now I had been able to get a full night's sleep
and, although I had just experienced a series of
very traumatic events, I felt completely sane. I
asked her, "Are you a Christian?"

"I am," she said. She thought for a moment,
then asked, "How did you end up here?"

"I'm not supposed to be here. Please pray for
me."

"I will pray for you," she said. "I have a
daughter about your age."

After she left, I napped until a staff member
came to ask, "Are you hungry?"

"I am, but not for anything like the breakfast
they tried to serve at the other place."

He brought me a packaged bagel, cream
cheese and a bottle of water. I thanked him, ate
and waited until he returned for the next
assessment.

"Why are you here?" he asked. (I wondered
the same thing.)

I explained all that had happened over the

past few days and he said I should write a book.

"That was the original plan," I said, but had no idea of the depths of this book.

He took my picture, put a patient band around my wrist, and led me to a physical examination room to assess the terrible cough from the flu I had been fighting for two weeks. I felt a bit better when another patient said I had the best photograph of everyone there. It was because I was the only one who did not arrive at the hospital drunk from alcohol or high on drugs.

The medical doctor was around my age, so I asked if he was a Christian.

"Who are you?" he asked, and this led me to quote some scripture. He was shocked by my curiosity and told me a bit about himself.

After finding nothing wrong with me, aside from the horrible cough, the doctor passed me on to the next staff member who showed me to the room where I would be staying. As we walked down the hallway she asked if there was anything I wanted.

Right then we passed a Bible on one of the tables, so I grabbed it close and said, "This book is the only thing I want."

"You can have it!" she said, then introduced me to my new roommate. When I saw the bed, after only one full night of sleep in six days, all I wanted to do was fall in and sleep.

I was still trying to process the many traumatic experiences of the past week: first the odd prayer meeting with Noadiah and her demands to lie, then the escape from Florida to safe haven in Georgia, then Michal screaming her betrayals at me, and another escape to a gated hotel, then to find police officers at Judas' apartment (another betrayal), taken in handcuffs and chains from the first facility to a psychiatric hospital, and no idea how long I would be required to stay. I had just walked through another very traumatic experience.

I put the Bible on the nightstand and started to lay down when another staff member handed me a slip of paper.

"You already got a phone call!" she said brightly.

I looked at the paper and softly set it aside. Michal's phone number. How did she know where I was?

Then exhausted, I turned over and went to sleep.

CHAPTER TWENTY-THREE

Revival Among The Broken

**"Will you not revive us and bring us to life again,
that your people may rejoice in You?"
Psalm 85:6**

A staff member woke me at 5:00 a.m. to
check my blood pressure, take my temperature,
and draw blood. I hate needles but I had been
involuntarily committed to a psych ward.
Refusing a blood-draw was probably not an
option. I gave her my arm and turned my head to
pray, then I realized it was over. Not that bad at
all. Then I went back to sleep until it was time
for breakfast.

Breakfast was not as dreadful as the one they
tried to serve me at the psychiatric assessment
unit. In fact, they had top-of-the-line food with a
sanitation rate of 100%. Even now I miss some
of their food, especially their mashed potatoes, as
well as their coffee I poured over ice cream
every night.

After a delicious breakfast I went back to the
room to read my Bible. I had started a thirty-day
Bible challenge to read forty chapters a day with
a few friends back in Florida, so I picked up
right where I had left off before I had been

literally sideswiped from all the trauma.

Later I went to the common area to get to know people and share Jesus with them. As I evangelized, one verse that revolved around faith stuck with me: *"But without faith it is impossible to [walk with God and] please Him, for whoever comes [near] to God must [necessarily] believe that God exists and that He rewards those who [earnestly and diligently] seek Him." (Heb. 11:6)*

I used this one verse with nearly every person I met during this psychiatric experience. I asked if they were Christians then reminded them of this verse, regardless of their response. This specific scripture burned within me the entire time I was in the hospital. I used it so much, I learned we do not have to be an eloquent speaker or quote the entire Bible to evangelize to someone. With this realization I was determined to focus on helping others rather than sit and reflect on all my own personal trauma. I had Jesus, but they did not. I took every opportunity to talk with those around me, asking if they knew Jesus, to the point where several asked if I was a Jehovah's Witness. I was like, "What? No! Far from it actually."

The hospital was open twenty-four hours a day, seven days a week, and the staff changed every twelve hours. New patients were admitted frequently, and I probably asked over forty about their relationship with the Lord during my ten-day stay. Right when I thought I had reached them all, a new person walked through the door.

From an evangelist's perspective, seeing a new person is like seeing a new fish. An evangelist fishes for souls. Remember where Jesus found the fishermen, Andrew, Peter, James, and John in the Bible?

After a few days in this co-ed facility, the constant flow of new fish became a little overwhelming; I was the only one ministering to both the patients and the staff. So after being among the other patients for several hours at a time I would purposely go back to my room to read the Bible and pray to replenish spiritually, then immediately headed back to the common area that had become my mission field. I was able to minister healing, encouragement, and salvation to many broken people.

Although the mission field grew faster than I could keep up, I loved it. Revival was happening inside of a psychiatric hospital and I had full reign to minister because I was a "psychiatric patient".

During my stay I ministered to people from all walks of life. Among them were recovering alcohol and drug addicts, gang members, homosexuals, the forgotten, depressed, adoptees, college students, single moms, single dads, divorcees, seniors, transgenders, and some who had attempted suicide.

We often want to go to other parts of the world to share the Gospel message, but God showed me an international ministry right where I was, inside of a psych ward. I had the privilege to meet people from various cultures and ethnicities, from Africa, Puerto Rico, Algeria, and the Ukraine.

This large mix of people also came from different spiritual backgrounds and denominations: Methodist, Baptist, Muslim, Buddhist, non-denominational, Wiccan, and of course, atheist. While ministering to so many different people I realized, not all, but most of them had a background with God, grew up knowing about God or had at least one family member who taught them about Jesus and prayed for their salvation.

I learned a lot there in that psychiatric hospital. I was able to minister to the broken, regardless of background, culture, or religion. I could easily relate to each one of them because I, too, was broken. The only difference was that I had a solution to the brokenness: Jesus Christ.

Medical Evaluations

Everyone admitted to the psychiatric hospital is required to see the psychologist there to have their medications adjusted to meet their own personal needs every few days. The psychologist is also the one to determine the discharge date for each patient.

At our first visit together he asked, as so many others had, "Why are you here?"

When I told him about my relationship with Noadiah, he was glad I had been able to escape her control. I was not prescribed any medications, but he warned I would get an immediate injection if he saw any symptoms arise while I was there. I knew exactly what he meant; I had already seen a patient get "injected" for acting out.

Our last time together the psychologist asked what my plan was when I left the hospital. By then I had decided to file a restraining order against Noadiah as soon as I walked out the door. She had been harassing my family in multiple states ever since my escape.

"I believe you had a mental breakdown from all of the post-traumatic stress you've been through," he said, "but I'm glad you got away from your ex boss and have a plan to execute once you leave from here." I thanked him and He arranged to release me as soon as he could talk with the hospital therapist who had been also working with me.

Before I left his office, he stopped me. "One more thing. A patient told me they're uncomfortable with you talking to everyone about Jesus and I suggest you keep what you believe to yourself."

Although he could not tell me who had said this, I was almost certain I knew. I told the doctor I knew how to be under authority, so if he wanted me to stop sharing Jesus, I would.

Back in my room I prayed to God, asking to be kept at the hospital as long as He needed me there. I thought about what would happen if God needed me there for months but chose to trust the outcome according to His will.

I continued to associate with those around me and play cards in the common area, but remained vigilant to keep Jesus from our conversations. Now, if the other person brought Him up, I played on what they said, and that was okay.

I maintained peace in a psych ward by reading my Bible and praying without ceasing. (1 Thess. 5:17) As I read that night there was a knock on my door. One of the girls stood crying, begging me to please pray for her little girl who had been taken to the hospital with a 102-degree fever. So we prayed together for her daughter. I knew this young lady had been admitted to the hospital due to a suicide attempt and ministered to her about how much her family needs her.

"What would've happened if you had died when you tried to kill herself?" I asked.

The psychologist had suggested I not talk about Jesus, but now the patients were coming to me. They asked for prayer because they knew they needed Jesus! I was not about to turn them away, nor would I stop praying. We are all in need of prayer.

The next day I learned my discharge release had been approved for Saturday, but due to a miscommunication between the psychologist and the therapist I ended up staying until Monday. Guess God wasn't done with me at the psychiatric hospital.

CHAPTER TWENTY-FOUR

Obscure Christians

"But are you willing to recognize, you foolish [spiritually shallow] person, that faith without [good] works is useless?"
James 2:20

A Christian, a follower of Jesus, is meant to be a bright light in the darkness. If a poll were taken of those who claim to be Christians and those who do not, the majority would claim to be a Christian. The shock factor comes when those who claim to know Christ have never shown any evidence to back up their assertion. This is what an obscure Christian looks like to someone who has never seen "good works" from a person who claims to know Jesus. God says our faith will be known by our works, but we do not get to Heaven based on our works alone.

Obscure Christians are those who hide Jesus for themselves and never share the gifts that have freely been given to them. If we are unwilling to share Christ with others, we are not being good stewards of all God has given us. If God thought enough of us to share His power, anointing, healing, and forgiveness, how much more does He desire for us to share our knowledge and revelations with those who are hurting? We benefit only ourselves when we keep our healing and restoration hidden.

God wants to bring His followers, His Christians of faith, to a place where He can use them as vessels to transmit His power and healing into the lives of others. We do God a disservice when we conceal the answers, understanding, knowledge, and healing that He made manifest in our lives.

Do not be afraid to share your story of how God brought you out of darkness and restored healing to your heart. Why hide your story when it has the potential to set someone else free from their misery? We need to be good stewards of all that God has given us to carry: *"But we have this precious treasure [the good news about salvation] in [unworthy] earthen vessels [of human frailty], so that the grandeur and surpassing greatness of the power will be [shown to be] from God [His sufficiency] and not from ourselves." (2 Cor. 4:7)*

CHAPTER TWENTY-FIVE

Testimonies

"For with the heart a person believes [in Christ as Savior] resulting in his justification [that is, being made righteous—being freed of the guilt of sin and made acceptable to God]; and with the mouth he acknowledges and confesses [his faith openly], resulting in and confirming [his] salvation."
Romans 10:10

I had so many revealing experiences during my time in the psychiatric hospital. One woman in particular stood in the middle of the common area, wearing a black hat, and screaming for hours. As soon as I heard her cry out, I knew she was under some kind of mental torment and knew I simply had to approach her with the antidote for her torment: Jesus Christ. I was scared, but as a Christian, we cannot allow fear to hold us back: *"For God did not give us a spirit of timidity or cowardice or fear, but [He has given us a spirit] of power and of love and of sound judgment and personal discipline [abilities that result in a calm, well-balanced mind and self-control]." (2 Tim. 1:7)*

I sat beside her at the table one day, asked if she wanted to play cards and there, over a game of Rummy, I learned about her life. She was in a homosexual relationship with a woman before arriving in the psych ward. Our conversation eventually led me to tell her about Jesus, how He died on a cross for sinners and rose three days later. When I asked if she wanted to accept Jesus into her heart, she reached out her hand with an emphatic "Yes! Like her life was dependent on it!" I took her hand and led her to Jesus. As soon as she confessed she was a sinner and repented of her sins, there was such a sudden dramatic shift in her countenance that I was shocked! This woman went from complete agony in her torment to the total peace of Jesus Christ.

How had it been so easy and fast for her to come to the Lord? When I first heard her screaming in the common area, I figured she wanted nothing to do with God or with anyone else, but she was desperate; everything she had tried before Jesus had failed. I later discovered her girlfriend had also been into Wicca.

The next time I saw the same woman she was in tremendous back pain. I asked if I could pray for God to heal her back and again she said, "Yes! Please pray for me." So I prayed that God would heal her and take away the pain in her back, then gave her a Bible to read.

A few days later, she came to me and said God had healed her of back pain when I prayed for her and asked if I would pray for another problem she was having. Of course, I was delighted. God was healing people both physically and emotionally in a psych ward! The power of Jesus is not limited to inside the church alone. In fact, we as individuals ARE the Church - Jesus lives within us. His power and healing flows through us no matter where we are!

I spoke with a young man shortly after his arrival and learned he had first been given a gun at the age of eleven, then he was trained to be a member of a street gang. He, too, accepted the Lord into his heart after I ministered with him a few days. I gave him a Bible and said, "In order to push out all the old mindsets and lies the enemy planted deep inside your brain, you need to renew your mind and heart with the Word of God." He carried his Bible everywhere he went, even the cafeteria, and every time I saw him reading that Bible, I realized another reason why God had placed me there for a short stay in the mental hospital.

This young man helped me learn something, as well. When he heard me tell a staff member there was a spill on the floor he said, "Don't talk to him as if he's your slave," and quoted scripture: "Jesus came to serve, not to be served." Then he got some paper towels to clean up the spill himself and, through his actions, he taught me to be humble in the Lord.

This made me self-reflect and realize he was right! I could have easily cleaned it up! So I apologized to the staff member and, after that, any time there was a spill on the floor I got paper towels and cleaned it up. There is no need to inform staff when I am perfectly capable of cleaning up a spill myself.

I am very thankful for the way God uses us to minister to one another. Not only did God use me to impact the lives of others in the hospital, He also used those to whom I had ministered to turn around and minister back to me. Perhaps our example of cleaning up spills in the facility inspired other patients to take more initiative for themselves.

This is how God can and will use anyone to impact us in His teachings. We only need to stay humble and teachable to receive what God wants to teach us through others. If we only focus on the negatives, we often miss the lessons and blessings God has planned for us to receive.

Delayed But On Time

The day of my discharge, hospital staff returned my phone and said Michal was there to take me home, but at the front lobby we realized she had not yet arrived. When I called, Michal said she would not be there for another hour, so I asked permission to join the others for lunch in the cafeteria.

Earlier in the week a guy had arrived at the facility covered with piercings who was dealing with much anxiety. I knew this from his first day and prayed for him often. Instead of joining the rest of us to eat in the cafeteria, he always chose a corner table with his back turned away from us. The night before I left, he had been reading in his room when he became so distraught from demonic oppression that he had forced himself to

157

come out among other people in the common area. There, I prayed with him to break his anxiety attack.

So on this day, when my departure had been delayed for an hour, he chose to sit next to me at lunch and promptly proceeded to have another anxiety attack as we were eating. I turned to remind him of our prayer the night before: "Only Jesus can take this feeling away from you. Are you ready to accept Jesus into your heart?" I reached out my hand and he put his hand in mine. I prayed with him to accept the Lord into his life and he did.

After lunch I stopped at the front desk where one of the staff members kept a stack of Bibles for me to share with the other patients. I took a Bible, opened it to Romans chapter 8, then walked over to give it to this guy to read. "Thank you for my new Bible," he said.

"Scripture speaks to each of us in our own ways, you know." I said.

By then, Michal had arrived. It was time to leave, but I knew there had been a specific purpose for the extra hour I had stayed.

"We know that in all things God works for the good of those who love Him,
who have been called according to His purpose."
Romans 8:28

CHAPTER TWENTY-SIX

Readjustment

"But I say, walk and live [habitually] in the [Holy] Spirit [responsive to and controlled and guided by the Spirit]; then you will certainly not gratify the cravings and desires of the flesh (of human nature without God)."
Galatians 5:16

Part of the discharge process included an agreement to return for outpatient therapy at 8:00 a.m. every day for the next ten days. I knew it would be good for me to be part of a group while adjusting to life outside the hospital, but Michal lived two hours away. Moving in with her was not an option anyway considering what happened the last time so, before I could leave the hospital, I had to find a place to live in close proximity to the hospital until therapy was complete. Michal suggested I move in with Ananias, Abner, and Samson at P.W.'s place, but I immediately rejected that idea.

"I'll just find some roommates and move into an apartment close to the hospital," I said.

"P.W. offered to pay the rent on an apartment for you until you get back on your feet," she suggested. I was thrilled with the offer, but why didn't she say that in the first place?

So we had a plan. I would get an apartment and commit to paying them back when I got a job, even though they did not ask me to.

"You know, it's probably not a good idea to tell your new roommates about your relationship with Jesus, Sabrina."

"What? How could you say that to me?" I was honestly shocked. "They will know I am a Christian based on how I live!"

Although Michal and Noadiah both have many great qualities their bad qualities far outweigh the good ones.

When Michal picked me up from the hospital, she said P.W. could not find me an apartment, so instead, he had paid for a hotel room five minutes from the hospital.

Meanwhile, I was testing the waters to see who was talking to whom behind my back, so when I asked if anyone had talked to a specific person, she told me no.

Hmm ... She just told me information she wouldn't have known unless someone had talked to that specific person. Thoughts were tumbling over each other in my mind, but I let it go. I had enough to process, and I just wanted to get away.

After leaving the hospital we immediately went to the courthouse. I knew I had Jesus, but I also felt that I needed the protection of the law before I could sleep. I had decided to file a restraining order against Noadiah for harassing both my adoptive and biological families across the country while I was under psychiatric care. I no longer had any trust for Noadiah because of

the untruths she was spreading against me:
"Sabrina needs professional help as soon as
possible. Sabrina is delusional! I hope she gets
the right medication she needs."

Noadiah was spreading false accusations! I
received professional help, but no one could
figure out why I was there, nor had they
prescribed any unnecessary medications. Maybe
Noadiah spread these lies to protect herself in
case I decided to tell anyone about my treatment
under her ministry. In fact, she is the one who
needs a psychiatric evaluation.

After filling out the papers at the courthouse
they sent me straight to see a judge.
"Unfortunately," she said, "to get a restraining
order we need to have an actual court hearing."

This was something I did not want to do. I did
not want to see Noadiah again under any
circumstances.

"I understand why you would not want to see
her in court, but to have an active restraining
order against her you both must be present in
court for a hearing."

Remembering the time I went to court to
advocate on Noadiah's behalf while I was
working for her ministry, it was important she
knew how serious I was now. If she had let me
go peacefully such drastic actions would not
have been necessary, but she needed to know her
days of manipulation and control were over. She
had already brought tremendous trauma in my
life and I was tired of the harassment. Why did
she continue to call everyone I know with her

false accusations and attacks against my character? It had to stop!

I thought back to the days when I had trusted and valued Noadiah's advice. I had honored her position within her ministry, but God only called me to be part of it for a season, not forever. Now I have a different purpose. When I realized she would never let me go to pursue all God called me to do for His glory, I knew I had to resign. Why would she not let me go?

Knowing the police would serve papers on Noadiah the next morning, a court date was agreed upon. Michal and I left the courthouse and, before dropping me at the hotel, we went for Mexican food. I apologized for all the confusion the day she called the cops, mainly due to my lack of sleep.

I still had many questions about Michal's role in what had transpired over the past couple weeks. If I had been thinking straight, I probably should have filed a restraining order against Michal at the same time as I did Noadiah's. She was very helpful at times, but other times there seemed to be ulterior motives. Was there anyone I could trust anymore?

That night at the hotel was the first outside of the walls of the psychiatric hospital, where staff checked on us every fifteen minutes with a flashlight while we slept, just to assure we were still breathing. Their safety measures made me feel safe and secure; I never had any trouble sleeping. In the hotel I had to readjust to sleeping without being watched, and I still had so much on my mind.

Before getting up the next morning to prepare for outpatient therapy, I turned on a sermon and it charged my spirit to hear worship music for the first time in ten days. I prayed before going for breakfast in the hotel lobby and, as I sat down to eat, I noticed an Asian woman sitting nearby. Although I felt God was leading me to speak to her, I really did not have time, but when I saw her again while throwing my plate away, I started a brief conversation before leaving for therapy.

I told her I was a Christian and asked if she was. She said she was, that being in three different car accidents led her to Jesus. I asked if she had any pain in her body; I wanted to pray for her. She said she did not have pain, so I asked if I could just pray a blessing over her and she agreed. After I prayed for her, she told me a very important financial nugget, and I immediately knew that was why God wanted me to talk to her.

When we feel impressed by the Holy Spirit to talk and pray with others, it is important to obey. We never know what we might miss when we do not obey the voice of the Holy Spirit.

Going to group therapy means one must talk about their feelings, which I hate but I did it anyway. I learned a lot, especially about the various types of anxiety our body goes through when they go into fight-or-flight mode.

As a past patient in the psychiatric hospital for ten days, I had a desire to work there so I applied immediately after my first therapy session. I knew their routine and was passionate to work with the broken. An employee did not carry the same flexibility to minister with others, but I could make a difference within the work environment, and any time God opened a window of opportunity for me to minister.

After a few days of therapy and a few nights adjusting to sleeping alone at the hotel, I quickly fell into a routine after all the recent upheaval in my life: Worship music to start my days, therapy sessions, quick naps, pick up food for dinner, then time to focus on my job-search and looking for apartments and roommates. Each day ended with a nice hot shower, my coping mechanism after going through so much trauma, watching sermons on YouTube, reading my Bible, and each night's sleep was more peaceful than the night before.

At therapy one day I asked a recovering alcoholic, with a five-year-old son, if I could pray for her later that day. She said, "Okay, please do." But when we stopped to pray at the end of the day, I did not feel as if that prayer changed much. *It could have been better*, I thought, but gave her a hug and promised to see her the next day.

Sure enough, she seemed to be in a much better mood at therapy the next day and her countenance looked very peaceful. She was excited to tell me about an email she received the night before about a job she had applied for several months prior. "I just know I got that email because you prayed for me," she said. The prayer I was so discouraged about and felt could have been so much better had caused her attitude to shift overnight.

Never underestimate the power of prayer and the simple words the Lord prompts us to pray. In the book of James, the Bible tells us that the prayer of a righteous man 'availeth much'. I was encouraged by what the Lord did in this young mom's life after I obeyed Him to pray what seemed like a simple, ineffective prayer.

We are the vessels Jesus wants to use to demonstrate His power. We only must be obedient to the Holy Spirit as He leads. You may hear an audible voice (I have yet to hear one), but most of the time you just hear Him in your heart, like an impression that leads you to do something or give something to another person. Hearing and obeying the voice of the Holy Spirit is a foreign concept to many. Due to all the noise of our world they do not understand. To hear God, we must get quiet before Him in His presence. This requires us to turn off and tune out all the noise around us so we are not distracted from hearing the still small voice of the Lord during our prayer time and throughout our day.

Back at the hotel that day, I kneeled beside the bed to pray, thank, and worship the Lord for His goodness and unfailing love. Just because I had experienced an overwhelming amount of trauma did not mean God was not worthy to be praised.

Another Wake Up Call

Michal called to say my mom was on her way to see me. At first, I thought Mom and Nabal were just going to stop in at the hotel on their way through town to visit Michal. Mom had married Michal's brother, so it would be natural for them to do this.

I kept thinking about my time at the psychiatric hospital when Michal often said, "I don't think it's a good idea for you to tell your Mom certain things."

Why, then did she now send Mom to my hotel without first asking me if it was okay? Can you understand my confusion over her wishy washiness?

Mom texted an estimated time of arrival: "I want to take you out for dinner so be thinking about where you want to go." All I could think about was mashed potatoes.

When she arrived at the hotel, I realized Mom had come by herself out of concern for me and we ended up going to Cracker Barrel for dinner. When we got back, she helped in my search for an apartment where I could live after therapy was complete.

"Whatever happens, Mom, please don't tell anyone where I'm living, especially Michal. If we decide to go see some prospective apartments tomorrow, please don't even tell her where we looked."

I no longer trusted Michal with any

information concerning my life, especially my living arrangements. She is the type of person who would hide out in the parking lot of my job, wait for me to get off work, and then secretly follow me home just so she knew where I was living. Just as the time Candace and I attended a Christmas party over an hour away and Noadiah suddenly showed up without telling anyone she was coming.

Since my Mom had come to visit, I decided to skip therapy the next day. We could miss up to three days and I needed her help to get my life organized. My car was still packed full of everything I owned from the quick Florida escape, but it was a complete mess from the police pawing through my belongings in search of the gun. The chaos and clutter in my car just added to my level of stress.

As we prepared to leave that day, I received an unexpected call from Dad: "What's going on? How are you doing?"

"My adoptive family all worked together to frame me, Dad, then the cops came, put me in handcuffs and took me to the psychiatric hospital."

"Who would do that?" he asked. "Who would go to the court to file an involuntary commitment on you?"

I was unaware there was a process where someone would have to go to court to have another person committed to a mental hospital. I had not even thought to ask how I got there. Trying to process the false accusations that had

been said against me was enough without also
trying to figure out who took legal action to have
me committed.

"I will find out and let you know after Mom
and I go shopping."

"It sounds like you have no support at all
down there. Why don't you just come live with
me?"

After Dad's phone call, Mom and I checked
out a potential apartment, then went to the store
for needed supplies where I sent Michal a simple
text: "Talked to Dad. I want to know who went
to court to get me involuntarily committed?"

I already knew the commitment was based on
the lie that I had a loaded gun in my possession
and was homicidal against Judas. I had seen this
much information on the $7,000 bill the hospital
gave me while I was still there, but who had
gone to the court to have me committed? Michal
acted as if she did not know.

Was it Noadiah? She was spreading lies about
me, claiming my urgent escape from her ministry
was due to my childhood trauma, thus breaking
the sanctity of privacy I had shared in total
confidence. Even though she insisted I needed
professional help, I had been cleared by doctors,
therapists, and a psychologist at the psych ward.
They said my mental break was due to extreme
stress, but they never saw the need to prescribe
any medications, not even for sleep, and not even
for anxiety. This all proved that Noadiah was the
crazy one, not me. Even so, I knew she had no
chance of having me committed since she lived

in an entirely different state.

The power of deduction led me back to Michal. Now I knew she had been lying to me as well as lying about me. She had lied when I questioned her about that certain person after she picked me up from the hospital, and she had lied when she told the police I had a loaded gun, threatening to kill Judas.

Everyone around me told their constant lies to make me feel as if I was going crazy, but I knew I was not crazy! Michal continued to beat around the bush with her half-truths until I was fed up.

"Just stop, Michal!" I finally said. "Stop! I already know the answer. I just wanted to see if you would tell me the truth, but you haven't."

No wonder I had fallen into manipulation and control under Noadiah. God was revealing patterns and cycles of manipulation and control that I had been deceived by my entire life.

Michal never did tell me the truth. It was Judas, the one they said I was homicidal against, who eventually called with the facts. He did not feel the truth should be hidden from me any longer. We always got along. The only thing we did not agree on was his decision to practice homosexuality, but I had so much appreciation to him for being honest with me.

I was done with Noadiah's spiritual and mental use and abuse against me. I was done with Michal's lies and false accusations against me. Just as Noadiah had used Martha as a pawn on her chessboard of deceitfulness and control, Michal had used Judas as a pawn to get me just where she wanted me. What would she do next? I did not trust her anymore.

I knew now. Ultimately, it had been Michal who had gone to court to have me involuntarily committed to a psychiatric hospital for ten days, under false allegations and false accusations. With this realization I sent Michal a simple text:

"Do not come near me. If you do, I will call the cops."

CHAPTER TWENTY-SEVEN

Escape #2

"Rejoice always and delight in your faith; be
unceasing and persistent in prayer; in every
situation [no matter what the circumstances] be
thankful and continually give thanks to
God; for this is the will of God for you in Christ
Jesus."
1 Thessalonians 5:16-18

After learning the truth of what Michal had
done, after trying to come to some sort of terms
about the abuse and control Noadiah had over
me, after all the false accusations, the lies, and
the trauma, I was overwhelmed. And with that, I
made one last phone call.

"Dad?" I cried through the phone.

"Just come to me and Grandma H. Let's try to
come up with a plan before you do anything
else."

I had been agonizing over where to go and
what to do next. They lived so far away, but it
might be the perfect solution. Just then I received
a Facebook message from Grandma H: "I feel
like you are not in a place to be working just yet.
Maybe you need to take some time off to rest
after all you've been through."

This made me rethink my current situation

before writing back: "That's probably true, but I have bills to pay." Every year that I worked for Noadiah and her ministry I racked up $1,000 in interest on my college loans since I put them into deferment.

She immediately wrote back: "Just come to me and your Dad. We will take care of your finances while you rest and recalculate."

What an unexpected blessing! I had just reconnected with Grandma H the previous year when my brother Solomon and I went on a road trip to visit both my adoptive family and our biological family for the holidays. Our Dad had been in and out of prison so much, we had only met him two or three times before then. For nineteen years I had barely known my Grandma H and here she was ... the one who had come to my rescue.

Receiving her message lifted a ton of pressure from my shoulders. It also made me realize she was right. My world had been flipped upside down and I was not in a place mentally to start working right away. It has never been easy to allow anyone to help me financially. I had learned that doing so only opened the door for them to eventually use it against me: "Look what all I've done for you! Look at what I've bought you!" I despised it and, because of that, I preferred to be dependent only on myself from here on out.

I had trusted Noadiah to help me financially but, just as Michal had done, when things didn't go according to her plan, she threw it all right back in my face. And then she called all my family, my friends and her associates in ministry to tell them about it, breaking a bond by disclosing my private financial situation, in addition to fabricating lies against me.

Now the Lord had offered me a new direction. And where God guides, He always provides.

When I told my Dad I had four more days of outpatient therapy, he said, "Talk with them. Explain your situation. Promise to continue your therapy here so you can come home tomorrow."

After discussing it with my therapist the next morning, she agreed to my immediate release, wished me well and provided the requested list of Christian therapists I could connect with at my destination. Then I got in the car and drove all the way to Missouri where my Dad and Grandma H were waiting for me.

As I was driving Judas called. "Where are you?" he asked. There was a sound of desperation in his voice. "Michal told me you and your Mom are on your way to the courthouse to say stuff against her. I just want everyone to calm down. This is getting outta control!"

Without mentioning my current escape route to Missouri, I said, "Calm down, Judas. I'm exhausted. I just need time to sort things out and recover from all that's happened. I assure you; Michal's statement is just not plausible."

Thoughts were swirling around my head like a wildfire. Judas didn't realize it, but he had just confirmed my decision to leave Georgia without telling anyone. It was best to keep my future plans to myself. If he made Michal aware of my decision to leave, she would probably have the cops after me again, telling more lies to take control over me. I just wouldn't be able to handle it.

I was beyond exhausted when I finally arrived. My car was still a chaotic mess from my various escapes, so I grabbed a blanket from the front seat and walked through the door to find Grandma H and Dad still sitting up, waiting for my arrival.

I gave them each a hug: "I wish I was here under better circumstances."

"I'm just glad you're here," Grandma H said. "You know where your bed is."

As I lay down in the most comfortable bed I had ever slept in, I was overwhelmed with gratitude and relief. After another long harrowing day, I closed my eyes and slept well.

I was home.

Recovery

I woke the next morning feeling safe and comfortable for the first time in months. It felt as if I had been holding my breath for years and now, I could breathe. Nobody knew where I was! Not Noadiah, not my adoptive family, and I felt free! When I left Florida, my vehicle was packed down with belongings, but half of my clothes were loaded into Michal's SUV. I lost many things in a short amount of time because of these two radical escapes, but I did not care. I was ready to start life all over again in a new state, far away from all the drama and trauma that had held me captive in the past.

I had just moved to a new location, to a new house, preparing to begin a new job and find a new church to attend. Everything was new, and for the first time I felt calm, secure, and content. I had escaped all the dysfunction, deception, manipulation, and control that had always been a part of my life. I was so thankful God led me to Grandma H's house. Even though I had no desire to live in her state at first, this is where God led me. I had found peace and contentment, and God was in control.

It is important to learn how to be content in every situation. Happiness is a feeling, but joy is a character trait that needs to be developed. Allowing Jesus to be our source of joy teaches us to be happy and fulfilled in every situation and circumstance because the joy of the Lord is our strength. When we face hard times, we need joy more than anything, even more than happiness. Happiness in a fleeting feeling, but JOY! Joy is a fruit of the Spirit that is anchored in the strength of the Lord. God deserves our praise no matter what we go through or how we feel.

There in Missouri I found rest after twenty-one straight days of chaos. I was extremely grateful to finally be able to rest, recover, and heal from nearly 25 years of abuse. After walking through all I had endured, it felt as if someone had forged me through a fire.

A month and a half of rest and recovery was ahead for me after settling in at Grandma H's house. It was finally time to allow myself to acknowledge my need for deep healing; it was far from a quick fix. Trauma, pain, abandonment, rejection, manipulation, control, betrayal, false accusations, and disloyalty had finally broken me. Acting like it did not matter, pushing it down or brushing it off as I had done my entire life was no longer an option. Nothing in me wanted to cover up or pretend the pain from the abuse I had endured did not affect me. I knew a fresh touch from Jesus was needed for me to live a happy, healthy life.

So in my place of solitude I began reconnecting with my biological family, praying, praising, writing, and fasting. I was close to my mom, just two hours away, and my aunt and uncle are only thirty minutes down the road.

After Samson tried living with Michal awhile, he moved in with our Mom. When that did not work, he quickly decided to move into Grandma H's house, too. Through Facebook we even connected with my little sister who was adopted at 10 months! When I finally acknowledged my hurt and need of emotional healing, Jesus began healing the deep wounds of my heart. The more I acknowledged my pain, the deeper my healing became.

I became stronger every day. Jesus is the great restorer of the broken: *"For I will restore health to you, And I will heal your wounds, says the*

Lord." (Jer. 30:17)

When Jesus restores and rebuilds us, He makes us better, stronger, and wiser than we ever were before the pain and trauma occurred.

My heart was still set on serving others, so after a time of recovery and walking through the process of forgiveness from the emotional abuse, I started working for a drug and alcohol rehabilitation center. There, the realization of how God uses His people wherever they are was even more evident. God can use us in any job or profession we pursue. We only must pray and be obedient to the leading of the Holy Spirit.

Since patients come from all over the United States to seek treatment for addiction, rehab is a major mission field. Those who have been broken often end up in a profession where they can give back to others because they themselves know what it is like to be hurt. They are the ones who have healed, who turn around and reach out an encouraging hand to pull others through the same stuff God has set them free from.

We break God's heart when we choose to keep our redemption story hidden from others due to some form of embarrassment or pride. To me, this is the ultimate definition of selfishness. When we choose to help someone else through their tunnel of pain and trauma to find freedom on the other side, God continues to restore us in ways we never imagined.

God tells us the harvest is ripe and the laborers are few because many do not want to share how Jesus delivered and set them free from the things that held them hostage. People who are bound to sin and addiction look to us to hold out a helping hand, to be bold in sharing our personal testimony and to pull them forth into a new freedom. We can give them the keys they need to open the padlock of chains that has been holding them in bondage.

CHAPTER TWENTY-EIGHT

Release

**"I have loved you with an everlasting love;
Therefore with loving kindness I have
drawn you and continued My faithfulness to
you."
Jeremiah 31:3**

Set Free

God sets us free from our pain, trauma, and suffering so He can use us to set others free from theirs. God does not waste our time but uses the things we go through to equip us with the knowledge and wisdom we need to help others who follow along the same pathway. We become stronger by properly processing our pain.

God has a reason for every season we go through. We must learn to shift our perspective to the bigger picture. Emotional pain and inner healing were always the number one place I feared going the most. Facing the emotions and pain that had resulted from the trauma I had experienced was a breakthrough moment for me. I wanted to be strong in the face of fear and pain;

I wanted everyone to see me in that light - STRONG. I have learned true strength is not afraid to expose and face the places that hurt us and caused us our deepest pain.

The places that bring us the most pain are the same places where God heals, restores, and truly sets us free. The best news is that we do not have to go to those places alone. God wants to be with us every step of the journey to inner healing, but we must first invite Him and His presence to come into our heart and life before He can bring healing to our deepest wounds.

God's healing completely restores our brokenness and pain if we are strong enough to give Him all our broken pieces, and not just a few. It is difficult to be real in the face of pain, but God cannot heal the brokenness until we are ready to be honest with Him about who we really are and how we really feel. God already knows everything anyway.

It is time to let go of all that has caused you pain and allow God to bring His healing to transform your heart, to reinvent you into the person He called you to be before you were ever in your mother's womb. *"Before I formed you in the womb I knew you [and approved of you as My chosen instrument], And before you were born I consecrated you [to Myself as My own]; I have appointed you as a prophet to the nations."* (Jer. 1:5)

Authentic disciples of Jesus focus more on allowing God to purify their hearts rather than focusing on being right or sharing only one side of the story. Their validation in Christ assures them of their identity, as they know vengeance belongs to the Lord: *"Beloved, never avenge yourselves, but leave the way open for God's wrath [and His judicial righteousness]; for it is written [in Scripture], "Vengeance is Mine, I will repay," says the Lord."* *(Rom. 12:19)*

God is love and therefore we must operate out of love, not out of our own agenda. The Kingdom of God is all about Jesus, not about us. Jesus made a choice to love others when they despised, mocked, and falsely accused Him, all while they spat on Him. He continued to love them, even when those who mocked Him nailed Him to a cross. He even went to the Garden of Gethsemane (It is a real place in Israel, I have been there) before going through the crucifixion to pray and ask God to take away what He was about to walk through: *"Father, if You are willing, remove this cup [of divine wrath] from Me; yet not My will, but [always] Yours be done."* *(Luke 22:42)*

Even Jesus did not want to experience pain or go through trauma, but He went through it because He knew there was a greater purpose. There will be no pain in Heaven, but even today - Jesus does not want us to feel pain. He wants to use both our negative and positive experiences to help someone else endure and learn from their pain. He wants to use us to shine a light in someone else's darkness.

Jesus humbly came to His Father and poured out His heart, but after He expressed His feelings, He was more concerned about fulfilling His Father's agenda than His own. Jesus chose to humble himself so He could conquer death, Hell, and the grave for our own sake. He was passionate about His love for people, and His heart ached for those who hurt Him: *"And Jesus was saying, "Father, forgive them; for they do not know what they are doing." (Luke 23:24)*

Do you know anyone who would pray for the forgiveness of those who had beat and humiliated them before raising them up on a rugged cross to be mocked in front of all to see? Doubt it. Jesus is the true definition of what it means to be selfless. Despite their critical comments, Jesus chose to ignore what people thought of Him. Jesus knew His validation came from above. He loved well because He knew in His heart that His Father loved Him.

When we truly acknowledge and believe we are loved with a never-ending love we will not be so quick to judge those who offend and hurt us when we are falsely accused.

Forgiving others is not easy. It takes the power of Jesus flowing through us to be able to truly forgive those who have offended us, and healing does not happen overnight, it is a process. We can say we are sorry and then have a negative thought about the person we just apologized to. True forgiveness requires us to use our heart, not only our lips. It is easy to vocalize "I am sorry", but it takes the work of the heart to bless those who have hurt us. *"Bless and show kindness to those who curse you, pray for those who mistreat you." (Luke 6:28)*

Christians whose relationship with the Lord is true, know they are required to do more than just read the Bible. We are also called to put what we read into action. Blessing those who have hurt us is difficult, at first, especially if we hold pride in our heart. Practicing what we read in scripture demands maturity by allowing God to cleanse our hearts of pride.

Forgiving Michal and Noadiah has not been easy. In fact, it has been the hardest thing I have ever done in life. Their false accusations and attempts to destroy my character and reputation were past my human ability to forgive. Yet I knew if unforgiveness, anger, or bitterness were lodged in my heart, I could not be an effective minister in the realm of influence God had called me to. Failing to address the unforgiveness and offense could easily open the door to a grudge inevitably developing and increasing in measure, and it is much harder to get free of a grudge than it is to forgive.

I quickly realized I did not have the strength that was needed to forgive. I had to depend on the Lord to give me the strength and wisdom to forgive Michal and Noadiah and when I did, my relationship with the Lord actually became closer. The greatest desire of my heart is to fulfill the destiny God placed within me, definitely more important than holding onto offense and anger.

God is love. God is not fake. God loves with a pure authentic love that cannot be matched. If our forgiveness does not restore and match the love of our Father, we have not come to a full realization of how much He loves us despite what we do. The love and forgiveness of God does not stop with us but extends to everyone we encounter, because we are all made in His image. Some of God's children have forgotten how much He loves them, so they act out of pride and emotional pain. It is difficult to think of anyone but ourselves when we are hurting, and some have become masters at hiding their pain. Many create a lifestyle of pain because they refuse to forgive the people who caused them their deepest heartache.

God restores our heart when we are mature enough to acknowledge that everything is about Him, not us. God desires our forgiveness of the other person, to be a representation of His love and character to those who have caused us to suffer. Someone may offend us, but we may be the very person God desires to use to show His great love for them. We cannot do this when we choose to harbor anger and blame in our heart and soul. We dishonor God by refusing to show mercy by forgiving those who have hurt us most.

All the pain that was stored deep within me felt like never-ending blows to my heart, but when I finally allowed myself to acknowledge that pain, I was able to pour it all out to God in prayer. Not only did God help me release the burden of anger, betrayal, bitterness, rejection, and loneliness, but He also restored and filled me with passion to love people like never before. I know what it feels like to be deeply hurt. I will not allow my heart to reflect the same hurtful actions of those who offended and treated me poorly. Identifying with the depth of God's love for me allowed Him access to my heart, to heal the deep wounds of betrayal and broken trust.

After that, I moved to the next step in my process of forgiveness: I wrote Noadiah and Michal each a letter, stating my forgiveness toward them and asking them to forgive me, as well. There are always two sides to every story, and we must be mature enough to recognize we all have faults. None of us are perfect; this is why we need a Savior.

Writing these letters expressing my forgiveness to Noadiah and Michal created a release within me that I did not expect; a release of pain, trauma, anger, bitterness, and unforgiveness once and for all. As I allowed God to heal me of the pain they had caused, I was able to bless both Noadiah and Michal in my prayer time, paving the way to close that chapter of my life. I addressed the letters to Noadiah and Michal, prayed over them and, without including a return address, placed them in the mailbox.

Forgiveness and closure are important. If we want to live a life of joy and experience freedom from offense, we must forgive those who persecute and offend us, even if they never forgive us. Closure, however, does not require reconciliation. Some people will refuse to change. Some do not see where they ever did anything wrong, but we do not need to let toxic people drag us down and continue to beat us up. Forgive them, yes, but do not allow your heart to be used and abused again. Narcissistic people will try their absolute best to guilt-trip us into feeling bad for drawing a safe boundary around ourselves to protect our emotional and physical health. Narcissistic people do not know how to respect the boundaries of others.

Noadiah still attempted to call even after I moved in with Grandma H and Dad. And just because I separated myself from Michal did not stop her from trying to threaten and intimidate me through social media, or drafting others to relay her message to me, mostly about publishing this book. Even though they continued to contact me I did not answer either one; their earlier actions had forced me to categorize them as people who are not safe for me. We are not obligated to answer every call or respond to every message, and there is no need to feel guilt for setting boundaries from toxic relationships. Enough is enough. When someone repeatedly refuses to treat you as you deserve to be treated, be wise enough to stand up for yourself and say "No". Sometimes choosing to remain silent and pray for someone can convey a louder message than trying to find the right words to say. Narcissistic people rarely change, and it is futile to try to fix anyone when they do not recognize their own faults.

Too many people today suffer some form of

physical illness that could have easily been
avoided if only they had chosen to forgive before
allowing their anger to turn into bitterness.
Bitterness causes us to develop a grudge, and
when we develop a grudge, our physical health is
at risk to develop all kinds of issues. Many do
not realize that everything we do affects our soul,
but the Bible tells us our physical health is in
connection to our spiritual health: *"Beloved, I
pray that in every way you may succeed and
prosper and be in good health [physically], just
as [I know] your soul prospers [spiritually]."*
(3 John 2:2)

CHAPTER TWENTY-NINE

Addiction

**"For God so [greatly] loved and dearly prized
the world, that He [even] gave His [One and]
only begotten Son, so that whoever believes and
trusts in Him [as Savior] shall not perish, but
have eternal life."**
John 3:16

Just as bitterness is a silent killer of one's
own dreams and desires so, too, is addiction.
Addicts become idol-worshippers when they fail
to put an end to the habit that has caused their
addiction: drink, drug, person, behavior, etc.

Picture addiction this way: You are going
fishing for the first time. You are sitting in a boat
in the middle of a large body of water filled with
fish but instead of catching a fish, you catch a
leech. You know various people who also like to
go fishing, but they have never caught a leech.
The leech you caught has captured your interest
though. You have never caught a leech before.
As you examine your leech, it jumps on you,
attaching itself to your skin, and starts sucking
your blood causing much pain. No matter how
hard you try to remove it, you cannot get it off
you. You did not want this leech to jump on you
but now you feel stuck with it. After all, you are

the one who chose to get in the boat and go fishing.

So you reach out to the other fishermen and attempt to explain the pain you are experiencing from this thing sucking your blood. Although they may sympathize with you, they do not fully understand what you are going through because they have never had a leech jump on them and suck their blood. Addiction is a deceitful trap that makes you feel hopeless while sucking the life out of you, leaving you for dead. Leeches are attracted to dead things, and when we do not know our identity in Christ, we are spiritually dead. Leeches are parasites that must attach themselves to a host in order to survive.

Imagine a drug being a leech that attaches itself to you. You realize it is not beneficial to your life, but you cannot remove it, and over time you realize it is slowly taking over your body and mind, making you lose control. The drug is acting like a parasite, taking you out by making you feel "less than" so it can gain full control over you, its host. Do not forget, the devil only comes to kill, steal, and destroy.

The number one commandment is to have no other gods before God: *"You shall have no other gods before Me." (Ex. 20:3)*

Anything we put above God is an idol that distracts us from Him. Why would we let the thing we are addicted to distract us from the person who knows more about us than we know about ourselves? *"But even the very hairs of your head are all numbered [for the Father is*

sovereign and has complete knowledge]."
(Matt. 10:30)

When we become addicted to our distractions, they can kill us both spiritually and physically. Addiction is not easily broken. Most of the time it feels like there is no way out of the living Hell the addict once willingly jumped into, no matter how hard they try to climb out. Most addicts do not enjoy their addiction; deep down they suffer from the guilt and shame they immediately experience after the high or "false sense of peace" fades away.

No one just wakes up an addict. The road to addiction starts when a person searches for satisfaction within their idol distractions. Once they identify with the "false peace" that alcohol, drugs, shopping, or food has been known to provide, they end up developing an unhealthy addiction that can never be truly satisfied. Drinking and doing drugs can destroy your body and your relationships, overspending can lead to debt, and overeating can lead to a myriad of health and psychological problems. That is why addiction is pure deception: it provides short-term satisfaction as it deceptively destroys your long-term satisfaction.

When I arrived at Grandma H's house in Missouri my Dad and stepmom were also living there, but soon decided to get a divorce. A few days after my stepmom moved out, Dad relapsed on methamphetamine in a hotel room. Meth, just like any other highly addictive drug, can cause insomnia. When we discovered Dad was hallucinating and had not slept in days, we had him admitted to a rehabilitation center to detox in a safe place. As we dropped him off at the facility, he kept apologizing to me.

"I am not the one you have to answer to, Dad. You need to repent and ask God for forgiveness, not me."

Repentance, like forgiveness, is not just lip service. True repentance requires a person to apologize, and then turn away from their sin. As a family member of an addict, it is difficult to watch those we love struggle with addiction, especially when it can be fatal. We must come to realize we are not responsible for the actions and decisions of others, nor are we required to carry the weight and burdens of their consequences, even when it is a family member. If we do, our life can become overwhelmingly depressing where we always expect the worst outcome. Looking at a glass half-empty is no way to live.

Exposure

Grandma H was scheduled for one of the painful surgeries delivered today: a full shoulder replacement. A few weeks before her surgery I dreamed my dad was sitting in our living room and said, "I'm using again"

Then I saw my stepmom in the kitchen saying something before I immediately told her to shut up and walked out of the room.

Upon waking, this dream carried a lot of

weight and I prayed for it not to be true. It continued to weigh heavy on my heart so as I prepared to go to work that morning I grabbed my phone to call my dad who was already at work.

When he answered I told him about my dream and asked, "Are you doing drugs again?"

He asked, "You dreamed that?"

"Yes, I dreamed that," I responded. Again I asked, "Are you using drugs?"

"No!" he said.

For a third time I asked, "So you aren't doing any drugs?"

Again he replied, "No"

"Okay," I said, "but I don't understand why I would have a dream like that if it were not true."

He again assured me he was not taking drugs, so I took him at his word. "Just take my dream as a warning, Dad."

Grandma H had her surgery on Thursday and released from hospital on Friday, quick because of COVID concerns. Doctors had warned her the recuperation period would be long and painful, so she came home with a pain numbing nerve block infusion pump, a controlled cold compression cuff and Oxycodone for the breakthrough pain. My stepmom had moved back in with my dad by then, so we felt comfortable someone would be at home all day to take care of Grandma H.'s needs.

I remained aware of my dream, but after Dad assured us he was drug-free, I tried to ignore the lingering concerns. I let it go until I came home from work four days after my grandma's surgery. As soon as I walked in the door I could tell something was bothering her.

"How are you, Grandma?"

"Oh, I'm in a little bit of pain. I confronted your dad earlier about some missing pills. I came home with 56 tablets and now I only have 21 left."

After we calculated the prescribed dosage required each day since she left the hospital, a total of 14 pills were missing.

"Well, I took three of them," my dad confessed to Grandma H, with my stepmom closely following.

"He gave me two pills to take."

When I found all this out, I was livid and quickly prayed for release from my anger. Grandma H is a widow! And now my dad was stealing her pain pills a few days out from a major surgery. The Bible instructs us to plead the cause of the widow, *"Learn to do good. Seek justice, Rebuke the ruthless, Defend the fatherless, Plead for the [rights of the] widow [in court]." (Isaiah 1:17)*

When my dad came back in the house I asked, "Dad, remember the dream I had?"

He gave me a quick "Yes."

"Well, why did you not take this dream as a warning?"

Remember my time with Ananias when I told him I would not tolerate alcohol? I quickly formulated a similar strategy for my dad.

Sitting a cup on the table beside me I said,

"From now on you will be taking a drug test." (Remember, I work at a drug and alcohol rehab.)

He walked right past me mumbling something under his breath as he shut his bedroom door.

Then I received a private Facebook message from my stepmom's daughter: "Why does my mom want to leave over there all the sudden?"

We thought my stepmom was already gone, but she had carried a lawn chair around the side of our house, hiding out there the entire time to avoid confrontation. After explaining to her daughter the injustice perpetrated by both my dad and her mom I walked outside to find my stepmom screaming to someone on the telephone.

She turned when she saw me: "Sabrina! I only took two Percocet *(Oxycodone)* that your dad gave to me. Your dad is stealing medication and money from your grandma, and he is selling drugs."

Stealing Grandma H's medication was enough for me to call the police but to learn he was also selling drugs prompted an immediate call to 911. I could not keep this information to myself. What if I found my dad dead on the side of the street? Or what if someone he was selling drugs to came to our home where Grandma H, Samson, and I lived? Knowing what my dad was doing, I would feel guilty for putting my family in danger if I did not speak up!

Did I want to turn him in? No, but what he was doing was immoral. It bothered my conscience to discover all this shocking information, confirming the dream that God had given me several weeks ago. I knew this dream had been a warning that my dad had ignored, and also lied to me about. I believed justice needed to be served. I was not about to cover up or conceal these immoral actions and behavior just because the offender was my dad.

At the same time, I immediately recognized how the devil was trying to pursue my thoughts. For a split second, the devil tried to make me focus on myself: If I choose to stay with my dad then I will have to deal with his drug addiction. If I chose to try staying with my mom and the codependent relationship she's already in with Nabal, then I would be forced to deal with an alcohol addiction. Neither side of the spectrum sparked my interest. I refused to come into agreement with the devil by allowing him to weigh on my emotions.

So I called 911. I spoke with the deputy and explained the situation, but they ultimately decided nothing could be done since they had no proof my dad actually took the pills.

I knew jail time would not fix this spiritual issue anyway. He had already spent many years in prison, more than enough time to resolve unethical behaviors and addiction, and it clearly did not work. After he was released from jail, he eventually fell back into the same immoral or illicit routines, which always led back to the same consequences that must be enforced: More jail time. Until we took care of the motives that caused the wrongful actions, doors would continue to open to develop cycles of misconduct. I did not think twice about reporting him, whether we share the same blood or not, and especially since he had been forewarned by a dream.

By reporting the injustice, even though they chose not to pursue it, my conscience was clear and my peace was restored. It was a difficult thing to do but it was the right thing to do.

When my stepmom's daughter showed up to take her away, my stepmom's parting words were, "If something would have happened, if the police had come here, your dad would have let me take the wrap. He doesn't even care about me."

I responded, "Most people who get in trouble with the law are only associated with those who actually commit crimes and they, too, are found to be just as guilty. The two of you, my dad and you, are in a codependent relationship." I knew my stepmom was not good for him because she hid all his secrets, and to enable an addict is to harm an addict. Plus she is an addict that is not motivated to change for the betterment of herself.

"I'm done!" she exclaimed. "We're divorced anyway." And with that, they backed out of the driveway and drove away.

After my stepmom left, I walked back in the house to discover Dad had indeed taken the drug test I had left on the table. And sure enough, he tested positive for Oxy. I cannot stress how important it is to pay attention to your dreams!

To be sure - Our sins always find us out. And if there is a prophetic person living in the house, chances are slim that anyone will ever be able to hide their injustice. After this, I began to see signs of manipulation with my dad as he avoided confrontation by giving us the silent treatment and isolating himself in his room.

Throughout this incident God had more mercy for my dad than I had for him. Although he was on probation, the police did not pursue any kind of legal action. God had just given my dad another warning.

The next day I sat with my dad on the front porch for a stern conversation. Strong boundaries must be set when dealing with an addict to keep them from manipulating and walking all over us.

"I want to be clear about my boundaries with you," I said. "I will not live in a toxic atmosphere. I left Noadiah and Michal because of their toxicity and I will also leave you. I won't even tell you where I'm going. Your 'wife' ratted you out. She told me everything you were doing with Grandma's pain pills."

"I did not sell any drugs!" he exclaimed.

"I believe you are a pathological liar." Then I tried to explain the only way he could find peace.

"You have a heart-issue that no jail will ever fix. You need to open your Bible and read it until you hear something from the Lord. God will speak to you, but you have to take action to hear His voice. You need to find a relationship with God, and you need to do it quickly before you end up back in jail. I won't stand for injustice, nor will I hide things just because you're my dad."

Then I said, "You know I called the cops on you yesterday?"

"You called the cops on me? What did you tell them?"

I replied, "I told them what I wanted to tell them"

He was silent, and so I continued. "There is no plausible explanation for you stealing Grandma H's pain medication."

"No. You're right. There's not," he agreed. "I will not let you treat her like that," I said. "And I don't appreciate being lied to either. Did you really think I was going to let you sell drugs with my little brother living in this house?" More silence from my dad. I closed with, "From now on you will take drug tests because we are running a rehab right here at this house. This is your sober living house and you are currently breaking the rules."Again he was silent. "It will be hard for you to hide anything from me because now you know ... God reveals things to me in my dreams. If I find out that you do one more thing, I WILL call your probation officer. Take this as your final warning." He did not respond so I walked back in the house.

About a week later, after staying in a hotel all weekend with my stepmom (toxic), he decided to move out. He sent a text to Grandma H saying he did not want to live with someone that threatened to call his probation officer. So him and my stepmom ended up getting their own place so they could be together.

We cannot allow someone else's addiction to cause us to become unhealthy by creating our own form of addiction to cope with the pain we feel for our loved one. This kind of mentality usually enables the addict to continue abusing the substance that already has them bound.

Addiction can feel like a dark, cloudy hailstorm that never ends. Never let the storm dictate your future, and never let your behavior toward the addiction become your identity. The devil wants to keep us trapped in guilt and shame. We must learn his tricks, learn to overcome the lie that we will never be good enough, that we are a screw-up who no one cares about anyway. This kind of thinking is wrong: "My addiction is only hurting me. I'll never be able to change so I might as well do it again."

Storms always blow over, no matter how difficult they seem in the moment. God factored in every storm we would ever have to endure when He planned our life. He knew we would not be strong enough to face all of life's challenges, nor could we overcome addiction all by ourselves. This is why God sent His one and only Son to die on a cross to pay our debt. We mess things up when we believe we are strong enough to embrace the storms of life or overcome our addictions without God. We make mistakes and we do not always know what the best solution is, especially in the middle of a cloudy storm. Jesus is not like us. That is why it is so important to have the spotless lamb on our side, because we are flawed.

Jesus is more real than the skin on our bodies. If we try to ignore Him now, we will be faced with Him again later. Death cannot be escaped and deciding to accept or deny the free gift of salvation is also inescapable. If we do not willingly accept Jesus' invitation, we inevitably deny it.

Right now you have a choice to accept the love and forgiveness of Jesus Christ. If you choose to neglect and deny Him while you are alive, you will not have a choice to accept Him after death. Why would anyone willingly choose to deny Christ when He only wants to reveal the depth of His love for us, heal our brokenness, and set us free from all that has tried to derail us from believing exactly who God created us to be?

Salvation is a simple gift. We only must believe in Jesus to receive it. Pray. Ask Jesus to reveal Himself through scripture. Confess that you are tired of striving to be good enough and that you want to accept His grace and forgiveness.

God does not want us to pretend we are a perfect Christian. He knows we are not perfect. That is why He sent His perfect Son to cover our sin debt. God desires for us to accept His invitation, develop a relationship with Him that ultimately sets us free from every distraction that has us bound by fear, guilt, and shame, and keeps us from the truth of His love. *"If you abide in My word [continually obeying My teachings*

*and living in accordance with them, then] you
are truly My disciples. And you will know the
truth [regarding salvation], and the truth will set
you free [from the penalty of sin]."
(John 8:32)*

***If you would like to give your heart and life to
Christ I want to lead you in this prayer now.
(Disclaimer: this prayer will not save you but
putting your faith in Jesus Christ and
confessing with your mouth that you are a
sinner and that you want to be forgiven, will.
(Romans 10:9-10). Pray this prayer where you
are.***

**Father I know I am a sinner and have let
my distractions, addictions, unforgiveness,
and selfishness lead me astray from Your love
and forgiveness. I believe that You sent Your
son Jesus to set me free and forgive me of my
sins when He died and shed His blood on the
cross and rose again for me. I pray that You
would forgive me and I ask You to come into
my heart to be my Lord and Savior. Thank
you for washing me clean, erasing my
mistakes and healing my heart from all of my
trauma. Guide me into your truth and help
me when I fail along the way, in Jesus name,
Amen.**

If you prayed that prayer with sincerity and
belief in your heart, all of Heaven is rejoicing
with you right now. (Luke 15:7) Welcome to the
Kingdom of Heaven!

CHAPTER THIRTY

How To Grow In Christ

"And do not be conformed to this world [any longer with its superficial values and customs], but be transformed and progressively changed [as you mature spiritually] by the renewing of your mind [focusing on godly values and ethical attitudes], so that you may prove [for yourselves] what the will of God is, that which is good and acceptable and perfect [in His plan and purpose for you]."
Romans 12:2

It is important to designate time each day to grow in Christ. I set aside one hour every morning, 30 minutes to listen to worship music while praying, and 30 minutes to read scripture. Am I perfect at getting up every single morning to do this? Not always, but there is no need to beat ourselves up for being so physically tired we miss our designated time with the Lord. Instead, let it act as a motivation to prioritize better, perhaps go to sleep earlier, or fast for a few days, to reset spiritually. Do whatever you need to do to get back on track with the Lord and remember always - Jesus loves us for who we are, not for what we do for Him.

Set aside time each day to spend with the Lord.

○ Consider spending half of the time reading scripture and the other half listening to worship music, giving thanks to God for everything, and telling the Lord what is on your mind and heart.

○ Daily devotions (YouVersion).

○ Write down what the Lord speaks to you in a notebook.

○ Read random scripture.

○ Listen to a sermon.

○ Join a Bible Study Group to focus on a specific topic.

○ The bottom line is just make time.

Never neglect prayer.

○ Prayer is your direct communication with Jesus.

○ Focus on His presence.

○ Holiness is a byproduct of time spent with the Father.

Become a student of the Bible.

○ The Bible is your instruction manual to become more like Christ.

○ True wisdom is gained through reading the Word of God.

○ Allow God's Word to teach and sharpen you so as not to become a stumbling block in someone else's story.

- o Do not read the Bible to preach it or teach it, read it to become more like Jesus.

Strive to become more like Jesus.

- o Do not allow your behavior to be the reason someone else misses Heaven.

- o Jesus can use His relationship with us to reveal His love to everyone around us when we become more like Him.

- o Your life is the only Bible some people will ever read.

Strive to be closer to Jesus and the Cross.

- o If you desire to be closer to Jesus and the cross, evaluate your life and sacrifice things that keep you apart from Him.

- o Acknowledge your need for Jesus in your life.

- o The closer we get to Jesus and the more we choose to sit at His feet, the further we are removed from sin.

- o Will you mess up? Of course you will. We all do. But healthy relationships become stronger when we have hurdles to jump over. (Jesus wants a relationship with you not a religion.)

- o *(Notice this does not say we will never struggle with sin.)*

Truly fall in love with Jesus.

- Invite Jesus to be a part of your life.

- Jesus is everything you need.

- He wants to be your best friend.

- Jesus promises to **NEVER** leave or forsake you.

- Lose the desire to do things that break His heart.

- Always remember you are <u>nothing</u> without Jesus.

- *"But there is a [true, loving] friend who [is reliable and] sticks closer than a brother."* *(Pro. 18:24)*

Be true to yourself.

- Know your values and set Biblical standards for your life.

- Be open-minded without believing and conforming to everything that is thrown your way.

- If we become an exemplary Christian on the outside and choose not to love others (even those who offend or treat us poorly), we miss the underlying concept of God's nature, and that is LOVE!

Let go of guilt and shame.

- The longer you allow guilt and shame to rule your life, the further you drift from God.

    o   Erase your agreement with shame to experience the fullness of God's love for you.

Forgive yourself and others.

    o   It is for your own benefit to practice forgiveness toward those who have hurt you.

    o   We cannot claim to be a Christian if we repeatedly choose to be emotionally imprisoned by unforgiveness.

    o   Freedom is a byproduct of forgiveness.

Get connected to a local church and stay connected.

    o   The Bible talks about how 'together' we all make up one body. *(1 Cor. 12:12-27)*

    o   The Bible also tells us not to forsake the assembly of others. *(Heb. 10:25)*

    o   Our unique individual differences help us grow into the people God has called us to be when we unite as one body in Christ.

    o   Every generation has so much to learn from one another, as well as teach one another.

    o   Everyone must work out their own salvation so do not be judgmental toward people who do not look and act like you.

Maintain healthy boundaries.

    o   Prevent pitfalls by paying attention to 'red flags'.

    o   Test every spirit in your corner so you will

not be side swept by betrayal.

- Learn to say "NO!" (Do not allow yourself to become a YES man.)

Choose now to follow Christ.

- Make a confession.

- It is unwise to teeter-totter between Heaven and Hell, as indecisiveness could cost you and those who look up to you for all eternity.

- He waits for you to call on His name.

- Jesus gave us a free will to choose.

- When we receive Jesus, we enter into a relationship (not a religion) that is sealed with an eternal covenant.

- When we accept, believe, and receive Jesus, we are redeemed from our past, present, and future sins. (This is not a grace card that allows us to sin, but a ticket to free us from condemnation as Jesus teaches us to deny our flesh.)

- Tomorrow is never promised. *"Do not boast about tomorrow, for you do not know what a day may bring." (Pro. 27:1)*

Allow the Holy Spirit to be your greatest teacher

"But the Helper (Comforter, Advocate, Intercessor - Counselor, Strengthener, Standby), the Holy Spirit, whom the Father will send in My name [in My place, to represent Me and act on My behalf], He will teach you all things. And He will help you remember everything that I have told you."

(John 14-26)

CHAPTER THIRTY-ONE

Restoration

**"I am the vine; you are the branches. If you remain in me and I in you, you will bear much fruit; apart from me you can do nothing."
John 15:5**

God never wants the trauma we walk through to become our identity, so He specializes in restoration. Nobody else has the right to identify who God created us to be, so we do not have to accept their thoughts, opinions, and insecurities. We get stuck when we accept the lies, so do not believe the lies that come straight from the pit of Hell. When people refuse to get on the same page with you, create a boundary. Do not let religious-minded people make you feel guilty for breaking ungodly, unhealthy soul-ties with them. The Bible talks about shaking the dust off our feet: *"Whoever does not welcome you, nor listen to your message, as you leave that house or city, shake the dust [of it] off your feet [in contempt, breaking all ties]."* (Matt. 10:14)

When Jesus died on the cross, He did not just die for your sins. The blood that was shed on the cross verified who He created us to be, despite the trauma we endure as a child, adolescent, and adult. God's love and sacrifice verifies us, and His blood redeems us. All you need to do is decide to accept Him into your heart and make Him Lord over your life. We do not have to live in shame and guilt, and if we let the enemy deceive us into doing so, we are living beneath the Kingdom identity Jesus bought for us on the cross. His blood acts as an insurance policy, as it shields us from all guilt and condemnation that comes from the evil one. When the enemy attacks, we only must believe we are covered in the blood of Jesus.

I loved Jesus before enduring all the trauma, but after He healed me of all that tried to break me, my love for Him became so much deeper. It is one thing to hear about the faithfulness, peace, security, and love of God; it is quite another to experience it for myself. In the midst of all the hardships, the pain resulting from the trauma of my past pushed its way to the surface and forced me to acknowledge it. It was my choice to properly deal with it. Processing the pain strengthened me and brought me so much closer to Jesus as He revealed a new revelation of His love for me.

The only reason (and I mean the ONLY reason) I was able to forgive Noadiah and Michal is because God deepened my understanding of His love for me. He loved me in my darkest hour, and this is how He wants us to love others in return. Despite how His children choose to act, every human being is created in His image. Noadiah and Michal hurt me deeply, but their behavior did not cause God to love them any less. When I chose to follow Jesus, I also chose to reflect His character. Was I supposed to stop being transformed into His image when I was thrown into a storm of betrayal, false accusations, and persecution? No! The storm made me stronger, as it deepened my faith to be dependent on Jesus and learn to abandon every part of myself to the One who is omnipresent, omniscient, and omnipotent (Psalm 139). I am incapable of doing anything apart from Him.

We will not develop a dependence on Jesus until we acknowledge we amount to nothing and are incapable of doing anything without our Creator. And we definitely will not develop any good character fruit until we learn how to sit at the feet of Jesus and dwell in His presence. Once we acknowledge our need for Him, we begin to realize how we will never reflect His nature and character, without His divine intervention in our life. When we realize this, we can transition into the transformation process to become more like Him.

If you want to be more like Jesus, you must be willing to sacrifice things in your life to make time to learn about His character. We are as close to Jesus as we want to be, as our sacrifice determines our closeness. Is it easy? No, the devil will try everything in his power to keep us from spending time with Jesus. The devil knows when we taste how good Jesus is, we will never stop pursuing Him: *"O taste and see that the*

Lord [our God] is good; How blessed [fortunate, prosperous, and favored by God] is the man who takes refuge in Him." (Ps. 34:8)

Our time and resources are never wasted when we invest them in Jesus. As we invest our time in Him, He reveals all the gifts and talents He has already invested in us. When we sow words of encouragement, we reap the benefits, *"for whatever a man sows, this and this only is what he will reap."* (Gal. 6:7)

When we sow words of discouragement, hostility, and judgment we reap those, as well. Our every thought and our every word will affect us, whether we choose to believe it or not. Words are seeds that take root in our life as soon as they come out of our mouth. This is why it is so important to guard our mouth: *"The one who guards his mouth [thinking before he speaks] protects his life."*
(Pro. 13:3)

CHAPTER THIRTY-TWO

Prophetic Fulfillment

"Now to Him who is able to do exceedingly abundantly above all that we ask or think, according to the power that works in us."
Ephesians 3:20

Noadiah once came to me during a revival worship service she hosted and said: "God told me your life has been like a dot-to-dot picture where the dots have been scattered, keeping you from seeing the whole picture. The final dot is your connection with me. Now that all the dots have been connected God is going to color in the picture."

Less than a year before I escaped Noadiah, the worship leader at one of her partnering churches prophesied over me one Sunday: "People have put ungodly expectations over you your entire life. God is about to open the cage that has you trapped and set you free. Your life is going to change dramatically over the next several months."

After this prophecy, I immediately sensed his words seemed to bother Noadiah: "You know, Sabrina, God already opened that cage and set you free from your childhood trauma when He placed you with me and my ministry. People should never give time frames when they prophesy over someone."

God gave me the title of this book: *Adopted, Transformed, Set Free* long before I ever escaped Noadiah, but the words *Set Free* were baffling to me. Then God reminded me that the prophecy spoken over me was not fulfilled until after I escaped from Noadiah and *Set Free* from the firm grasp she had on me.

You must understand, leaving Noadiah and escaping from her ministry was nowhere in the agenda. I thought God was going to transition me right there within her ministry. Then I realized God had been trying to tell me to transition for many months before I decided to actually move my feet. God's ideas and plans hardly ever resemble what we have pictured for our lives. God always exceeds our expectations.

Prophecy does not fulfill itself; we must move our feet to fulfill what God has spoken over us. When a prophecy has been spoken, we cannot just wait around for God to make it come to pass if we have not taken the appropriate steps to meet the requirements of its fulfillment.

Before leaving Noadiah's ministry, I prayed God would add everything to my plate that He wanted on it (scary prayer), and to take away everything He did not want on my plate for that season. I am still at a loss for words by the way God shook up and shifted my life in an entirely different direction after praying this prayer. That one prayer changed my life. Through that one prayer, I was *Set Free.*

Never underestimate the power of prayer. God

hears everything we say. He may not always answer in the way we want Him to but always remember: It is not about us; it is about God and He always answers our prayers. I am incredibly grateful for all the prayers I thought He did not answer. He knew what He had waiting for me in my future was better than what I could see in the present. He is a good Father who is intentional about every detail of our lives. His goal is to protect us, and sometimes we need protection from ourselves. We only have the ability to see the exterior of a situation and a person, but God sees the interior of each person's heart. His wisdom reveals things to us that our natural eyes could never see.

If you feel you are in a bad situation, if your peace is being disturbed, pray until God restores your peace. He may ask you to leave the situation, or He may ask you to change something about yourself. Either way, it is always best to adhere to God's guidance, as He knows what is best for us in every situation.

There came a point where I had a weird feeling every time I prayed over Noadiah in the prayer circle. After each prayer meeting, I personally prayed for God to create in me a clean heart and renew a right spirit within me. I did not jump ship and tell God I was done, to justify the situation. God is all about the heart and our hearts always reveal our true character. If something feels wrong, trust God to make a way when there seems to be no way out. *"I will even make a way in the wilderness and rivers in the desert."* (Is. 43:19)

The Holy Spirit never leads us astray or down a path toward destructiveness. Instead, when we focus on the Holy Spirit and tune into what He is saying, He pulls us out of any malicious circumstances we ourselves may be completely oblivious to. This is how faithful our Heavenly Father is and His love toward us.

A Prayer From The Author

Every word of this book was birthed from the
acknowledgment and healing process of my
personal pain and trauma. After finding healing and
restoration through prayer and devotion to God I
could not help but share it with the world. My
prayer is that my life story and personal relationship
with the Lord has been an encouragement to you. At
the same time, I pray God will pave the way for
your own emotional healing and personal freedom
from everything and everyone the devil has used to
make you "think" you are broken beyond repair.

Be blessed. Stay encouraged. Continue to fight the
good fight of faith. Always remember Jesus loves
you. He does not want you to live in physical,
mental, emotional, spiritual, or financial bondage.

Please take time to acknowledge, process, and allow
God to bring healing to your dormant pain. He can
restore you and prepare you to live a prosperous life
that reflects the same hope and healing to every
person in your story. When you truly experience
healing, restoration, and freedom you will not be
able to keep it to yourself! There is a warrior inside
each one of us. Do not let fear, a negative mindset,
or the opinions of others keep you from discovering
your true strength that will lead to your
breakthrough! Now go find your healing and
restoration!

And they overcame and conquered him because of the blood of the Lamb and because of the word of their testimony, for they did not love their life and renounce their faith even when faced with death.

Revelation 12:11

ABOUT THE AUTHOR

Sabrina Martinelli was nearly aborted before living through multiple homes in the foster system and adopted at age eleven. She holds a B.S. degree from Regent University and, with much experience in outreach ministry, shares traumatic personal experiences to help others find hope and healing. Sabrina loves the beach and anything that gives an adrenaline rush. She resides with family in Kentucky. Contact her at:
www.fb.me/AdoptedTransformedSetFree.com

Made in the USA
Coppell, TX
22 October 2020